Interpreting the Bible & the Constitution

Interpreting the
Bible
&
the
Constitution

Jaroslav Pelikan

A John W. Kluge Center Book
Library of Congress, Washington, D.C.

Yale University Press   New Haven and London

Published with assistance from
the Louis Stern Memorial Fund.

Designed by Sonia L. Shannon.
Set in Galliard type by Binghamton Valley Composition.
Printed in the United States of America.

Library of Congress Cataloging-in-Publication Data

Pelikan, Jaroslav Jan, 1923–
    Interpreting the Bible and the Constitution / Jaroslav Pelikan.
        p.   cm.
"A John W. Kluge Center book."
Includes bibliographical references (p.   ) and indexes.
    ISBN 0-300-10267-4
1. Bible—Criticism, interpretation, etc.—History. 2. Constitutional
law—United States. I. John W. Kluge Center (Library of Congress)
II. Title.
BS500 .P45 2004
220.6'01—dc22

                                          2003023274

A catalogue record for this book is available
from the British Library.

The paper in this book meets the guidelines
for permanence and durability of the
Committee on Production Guidelines for
Book Longevity of the Council on Library Resources.

10 9 8 7 6 5 4 3 2 1

In memory of Edward Hirsch Levi (1911–2000)

The influence of constitution worship. . . . gives great freedom to a court. It can always abandon what has been said in order to go back to the written document itself. It is a freedom greater than it would have had if no such document existed. . . . A written constitution must be enormously ambiguous in its general provisions. . . . A constitution cannot prevent change; indeed by permitting an appeal to the constitution, the discretion of the court is increased and change made possible.

—*An Introduction to Legal Reasoning*

Contents

Preface

As I have explained in the "personal introduction" to the first
chapter, this book is the outgrowth of my lifelong study in the
history of biblical interpretation, as amplified more recently by
my consideration of the analogy between this history and the
history of constitutional interpretation.

Several lectureships over the past ten years have given me the
opportunity to organize my reflection on this analogy further:
appointments at the University of South Carolina ten years apart,
as Knowlton Scholar in 1993 and as Beacham-Hall Lecturer in
2003; the inaugural Colman J. Barry Lecture at Saint John's University, Collegeville, Minnesota, in 1995; a lecture at Woods Hole,
Massachusetts, in 1999; my designation as the first John W. Kluge
Scholar at the Library of Congress in 2001–2, including a Kluge
Public Lecture on 24 September 2002 to members of the Madison Council and the Scholars' Council; the Philip McElroy Lecture on Law and Religion at the University of Detroit Mercy
School of Law in 2003 for chapter 3; and then, for the entire
book, the joint invitation of the Yale Law School and the Yale
Divinity School also in 2003. On each of these occasions, I have
had the benefit of comment and criticism from colleagues who
study the interpretation of the Constitution or from those who
study the interpretation of the Bible. I have also benefited from

the comments of anonymous readers of the manuscript for Yale University Press, who spotted a few mistakes that were relatively trivial but potentially embarrassing.

Involving as it does two distinct interpretive communities in the academy, in each of which scholarly writing over the years has evolved its own special system of citation, this book seeks to blend the two methods:

In citing my two primal texts, the Bible and the Constitution, I have followed the standard systems set down in *The Chicago Manual of Style* (14th ed.): for the Bible, 14.34–37; for the Constitution, 15.367 and 16.172 (employing the "Literal Print" authorized by the Eighty-third Congress in 1961, with its distinctive spelling, capitalization, and punctuation), including the provision that ordinarily such references be "made in running text" rather than in footnotes, which I have applied to both the Bible and the Constitution. Quotations of the English Bible are from the Revised Standard Version (RSV) unless otherwise identified as being from the Authorized ("King James") Version (AV), the New English Bible (NEB), or the New Jerusalem Bible (NJB).

For Supreme Court opinions, I have adopted the conventional system as described in the *Chicago Manual* (15.369–71), except that I give only the actual page of the quotation or reference, not the opening page of the entire case. In the interest of aesthetic symmetry — if not exactly of "equal protection" (amend. 14, sec. 1) — I cite councils, synods, creeds, and confessions of faith by a similar system: 1.8 *Westminster Confession,* 2 Creeds 607–8 (1647). "Creeds" refers to *Creeds and Confessions of Faith in the Christian Tradition, Credo* to my companion volume for that set, and *Christian Tradition* to my five-volume work, *The Christian Tradition: A History of the Development of Doctrine* (see Bibliography). But in referring to secondary scholarly literature, regardless of field, I have stayed with my usual "author-date" system of citation for both journals and books.

Although I capitalize such titles as First Amendment and Epistle to the Romans, I do not follow the custom in both communities of a wholesale capitalization of names for doctrines (Coinage Clause, Real Presence). For dates, spelling of proper names, and general information and bibliography, I have relied on *The Oxford Dictionary of the Christian Church* (3d ed.) of 1997 (*ODCC*) and on its judiciary counterpart, *The Oxford Companion to the Supreme Court of the United States* of 1992 (*OCSC*).

I am grateful to James H. Billington, Librarian of Congress, and to Prosser Gifford, Director of Scholarly Programs, for designating this the first "John W. Kluge Center Book, Library of Congress."

This book is dedicated to the memory of my longtime friend and colleague, Edward Hirsch Levi (1911–2000), who was Dean of the Law School, then Provost, then President, of the University of Chicago, and subsequently Attorney General of the United States in 1975–76, as well as, from 1986 to 1989, President of the American Academy of Arts and Sciences, the office in which I succeeded him from 1994 to 1997.* This dedication is a recognition of him as in a special sense *doctor utriusque iuris,* who, as the grandson of rabbis, proved himself faithful to this distinguished heritage by serving as a mentor to several generations of lawyers as well as of non-lawyers (including this non-lawyer) on the science and the art of legal reasoning and constitutional interpretation.

---

*I had the privilege of paying a memorial tribute to Edward H. Levi in the *Bulletin* of the Academy for May–June 2000, pp. 16–19.

Interpreting the Bible & the Constitution

Normative Scripture— Christian and American

The law his meditation night and day (Ps 1.2 NEB)

A Personal Introduction

In spite of my own preferences and contrary to my long-standing wont, I have let myself be persuaded, by those who ought to know, that it would be appropriate to begin this seemingly unlikely (perhaps even presumptuous) investigation with a personal note of explanation of why it does not at all represent the attempt of a historian of Christian doctrine to retool himself into a constitutional lawyer, but a continuity of interest and even of methodology. For in an academic variant on the familiar come-on line, "So what's a nice person like you doing in a place like this?" students, colleagues, and friends have repeatedly asked me— sometimes "challenged" would probably be more accurate—to justify why a cultural and intellectual historian whose bibliography includes monographs on a broad range of literary and philosophical texts, from Plato's *Timaeus* to Goethe's *Faust,* should have devoted the greater part of a long scholarly career to the unfashionable enterprise of editing, translating, and interpreting the creeds, confessions, and biblical exegesis of the church. This began in 1946 with a dissertation that included the first English translation of *The [First] Bohemian Confession* of 1535 (although the translation itself was not printed until 2003). To those questioners who identify themselves with the mainstream of the Christian tradition, I have often responded with one of my favorite quotations from Cardinal John Henry Newman's *Apologia pro vita sua* (which may, for that matter, be more true of me than it was of him): "I have changed in many things: in this I have not. From the age of fifteen, dogma has been the fundamental principle of my religion: I know no other religion." But when others, who stand outside that tradition or who identify themselves as "secular humanists," have pressed me about the nature of "dogma" as the normative teaching of the church in relation to the doctrinal authority of the Bible, I have found that the most helpful analogy for it is the authority of the United States Constitution in American society and its complex relation to the standing of the Supreme Court of the United States as its official and decisive interpreter.

The parallel between the two is, of course, far from being my own discovery. For example, a well-known study published by the distinguished constitutional scholar Edward Corwin in 1959, *The "Higher Law" Background of American Constitutional Law*, opens with the sentence: "The Reformation superseded an infallible Pope with an infallible Bible; the American Revolution replaced the sway of a king with that of a document." But most considerations of this parallel have, for understandable and valid reasons, focused on the question of the authority of the two texts rather than on the question of the proper methods for interpreting them. This question of the analogy between the methods of interpreting the two Scriptures, Christian and American, was especially on my mind during the years when I was preparing, in collaboration with Valerie Hotchkiss, a critical edition, in four volumes (including as one volume my historical and theological introduction, entitled *Credo*), of *Creeds and Confessions of Faith in the Christian Tradition*. The examination of the use of the Bible in these creeds and confessions, and then of the use of these creeds and confessions themselves in the life of the churches, made me reflect on the issues that in two chapters of *Credo* I called "Confessional Rules of Biblical Hermeneutics" and "Rules of Confessional Hermeneutics." There is a direct continuity between that inquiry and this one, which compares the several versions of official hermeneutics that the councils and confessions of the church over the centuries have applied to Christian Scripture with the several versions of official hermeneutics that the Supreme Court over the centuries has applied to American Scripture. For example, it was the application of the constitutional and legal categories of enactment, ratification, and enforcement to the functioning of the doctrinal authority of creeds and confessions of faith in the various churches that gave me the framework for a study of the authority of "Creed as Church Law," which puts into a larger context the clouded issues related to the requirement of "confessional subscription" as a test of orthodoxy and to the processes of conciliar, creedal, and confessional "reception."

Then, on 1 July 2002, the Annenberg Foundation Trust at Sunnylands and the Oxford University Press appointed me the Scholarly Director of their joint "Institutions of Democracy" project. Although this appointment came as something of a surprise to some — including, I confess, to myself at first — my preparation for taking on this unusual assignment has in fact been both scholarly and administrative. On the scholarly side, the project has become an ideal vehicle for this long-standing interest of mine in the analogies between biblical and constitutional hermeneutics, which is acquiring a new relevance for me, and, I hope, new substance and depth as well. On the administrative side, I was the dean of the Graduate School of Arts and Sciences at Yale (1973–1978), later the president of the American Academy of Arts and Sciences (1994–1997), and then the president of the American Academy of Political and Social Science (2000–2001). Through these associations I had come to know the work of many of the scholars who are now participating in the Sunnylands Institutions of Democracy project, and I learned that providing scholarly leadership for a cooperative academic enterprise can be rewarding and productive. I have benefited enormously — as a person, as a citizen, and as a scholar — from the opportunity to carry on my private education in public by listening to and reading the distinguished colleagues, especially from political science, law, education, communication, and American history, who have been contributing to this large-scale project, and thus also, at least indirectly, to this modest essay.

Great Code

There is a familiar and venerable text, centuries old by now, which is the product of multiple authorship (although even after generations of historical research and literary analysis we are not always in a position to determine with absolute precision just who wrote, or rewrote, which parts of it). The text was originally composed under very specific circumstances, which modern historical scholarship has done much to illumine. But far transcending the history of its original composition is its official standing ever since, for it has been adopted by a community as its normative Great Code, and therefore as occupying a position that in some profound sense stands beyond its own history: in Ralph Waldo Emerson's fighting words of 1838, "not spake but speaketh!" That normative status is based on the assumption that it can be applied to any and all of the radically changed situations of later times, many of which the writers who originally framed it could not themselves conceivably have foreseen. Every official action of the community thus has had the obligation of conforming to it, or any rate of not violating it, and of demonstrating that conformity when challenged to do so; and members of the community are under the strictest possible obligation to obey it. Therefore its words and phrases have for centuries called forth meticulous and sophisticated—and sometimes painfully convoluted—interpretation, as well as continual reinterpretation. By now, this interpretation has grown into a massive corpus of authoritative, if often controversial, commentary. Yet the text does not itself prescribe the method of such interpretation; nor does it specifically identify the authoritative agency that bears the ultimate responsibility for determining the binding interpretation, much less for revising it.

As it stands, that Ciceronian period would accurately describe both Christian Scripture and American Scripture, both the Bible of the Christian Church and the Constitution of the American Republic. Both of these texts are certainly "familiar." Indeed, their words and phrases have become so much a part of our vernacular speech that those who use them are often unaware of where they were said first. Although such sayings have become proverbial (and some of them may also have originated as proverbs), "a house divided against itself" appeared in the Gospels (Mk 3.25) and was being quoted from that source long before it was invoked in 1858 by Abraham Lincoln, to whom it is often attributed; and "by the skin of my teeth" is from the Book of Job (Jb 19.20). In the "ordinary language" of Americans, such phrases as "full faith and credit" (art. 4, sec. 1) and even "due process" (amend. 5) seem to have acquired a generalized meaning that is sometimes quite independent of their appearance in the Constitution. Conversely, words from everyday language have acquired a very specialized meaning from the way they are used in one or the other of these two texts. Chapters in a seventeenth-century confession of the Dutch Reformed Church bearing headings such as "A Single Decision of Election" or "Election Unchangeable" have nothing to do with political campaigns or vote counts, but with "election" understood as divine predestination, because of New Testament usage, including the admonition "Give diligence to make your . . . *election* sure, for if ye do these things, ye shall never fail" (2 Pt 1.10 AV). Because of constitutional usage, the Fifth Amendment provision, "nor shall private property be *taken* for public use, without just compensation" (amend. 5), has contributed to the vocabulary a special meaning for "taking," as in the epigram of Justice Oliver Wendell Holmes, Jr., "If regulation goes too far it will be recognized as taking," or even the plural "takings," as a name for the more specifically legal term "eminent domain," which goes back at least as far as Hugo Grotius. Such constitutional usage has made it possible for Thurston Greene and his colleagues in 1991 to compile a massive lexicon of the Constitution in a thousand pages, and for Albert P. Blaustein to prepare *The Bicentennial Concordance,* both of which bear a strong family resemblance to the basic reference works of biblical scholarship.

Both texts are centuries old by now, whether two or twenty, and both are "venerable" and even venerated and enshrined. As the fathers of the Second Vatican Council put it in their *Decree on Ecumenism,* "love and *reverence, almost a cult,* for Holy Scripture leads our [separated Protestant] brothers and sisters to a constant and expert study of the sacred text," which in the *Dogmatic Constitution on Divine Revelation* of that council Roman Catholics were urged to emulate. To attend the opening session of the Supreme Court is to witness a solemn ceremony, almost a kind of secular liturgy, complete with the symbols of ritual, incantations, and vestments. In a description that the Court itself provided in a decision regarding religious exercises in public schools, "The sessions of this Court are declared open by the crier in a short ceremony, the final phrase of which invokes the grace of God." Therefore, as Justice William O. Douglas once joked in another such case, "A fastidious atheist or agnostic could even object to the supplication with which the Court opens each session: 'God save the United States and this Honorable Court.' " With the reduction in the private authority of Christian Scripture, and especially in its public authority, American Scripture has been called upon to fill some of the gap. At least for some Americans, therefore, the Ten Amendments of the Bill of Rights now seem to provide a version of the function that used to be performed for their grandparents by the Ten Commandments of the Decalogue—with the arts often being called upon to provide them with a substitute for the mystical experience of divine transcendence. As Thomas C. Grey has put it, "America would have no national church . . . ; yet the worship of the Constitution would serve the unifying function of a national civil religion."

More functionally, the Bible was taken to be "profitable for teaching, for reproof, for correction, and for training in righteousness, that the man of God may be complete, equipped for every good work" (2 Tm 3.16–17); and the Constitution was likewise, in a description by Chief Justice John Marshall that was to become axiomatic for the Supreme Court ever after, "intended to endure for ages to come, and consequently, to be adapted to the various *crises* of human affairs." Although "source" and "norm" can sometimes stand in a coordinate position in the definition of the authority of Christian Scripture, it is helpful for the historical examination both of Christian Scripture and of American Scripture to distinguish between them. For although the historical sources of laws and of doctrines have been many and varied, each of these texts has been adopted by its community as its norm, in the expectation that in those "ages to come," with all their "various crises of human affairs," it would continue to be applicable to all kinds of crises and needs, many of which, in the words of Justice Holmes, "could not have been foreseen completely by the most gifted of its begetters." Consequently, as Justice Joseph McKenna summarized,

> Time works changes, brings into existence new conditions and purposes. Therefore a principle to be vital must be capable of wider application than the mischief which gave it birth. This is peculiarly true of constitutions. They are not ephemeral enactments, designed to meet passing occasions. . . . In the application of a constitution, therefore, our contemplation cannot be only of

what has been but of what may be. Under any other rule a constitution would indeed be as easy of application as it would be deficient in efficacy and power. Its general principles would have little value and be converted by precedent into impotent and lifeless formulas. Rights declared in words might be lost in reality.

It is probably supererogatory to point out that all of this, not least the danger of confusing "words" with "reality" and of reciting "impotent and lifeless formulas," is also "peculiarly true" of the Bible and its adherents.

"In Accordance with the Scriptures"

The most universally accepted of all Christian creeds — usually, though not quite accurately, called *"The Nicene Creed"* — affirms that the resurrection of Christ took place "in accordance with the Scriptures." This New Testament formula (1 Cor 15.4) refers most directly to various passages of the Old Testament — which is what the term "Scripture [*graphē*]" means in the New Testament — that are said to have prophesied the death and resurrection and that are said now to have been fulfilled; in fact, in some passages of the Gospels (for example, Mt 26.54–56) it almost sounds as though the very purpose of an event in the life of Jesus had been to fulfill a passage of the Old Testament Scripture. But "according to [*kata*] the Scriptures" has, of course, an unavoidably normative connotation as well, which is why "in accordance with" is often preferable to "according to" as a translation of the Greek preposition. For Christian Scripture above all, and also American Scripture, are not merely ancient and intellectually interesting texts, but each of them is, for its own community, uniquely "normative" and authoritative. As a result, in Robert Burt's words, "there are . . . parallels between the secular authority of the Constitution in the polity and the divine authority of the Gospels in religious belief, and between the exegetical role of judges and of priests and prophets. There is a further, presentational similarity between the Gospels' teachings and the pages of the *United States Reports*. In both settings, the claim for authority often appears apodictic, assumed rather than argued for, and deference thus seems commanded rather than requested." In words that the Supreme Court once called "language of the Constitution . . . too plain to admit of doubt or to need comment," therefore, the Constitution prescribes apodictically, and with no exceptions: "This constitution . . . shall be the supreme law of the land; and the judges in every state shall be bound thereby, any thing in the constitution or laws of any state to the contrary notwithstanding" (art. 6). The same authority extends to any subsequent amendments, which "shall be valid to all intents and purposes, as part of this constitution" (art. 5). And in the aftermath of the Civil War, Abraham Lincoln's friend and sometime campaign manager, Supreme Court Justice David Davis, declared, speaking for the Court: "The Constitution of the United States is a law for rulers and people, equally in war and in peace, and covers with the shield of its protection all classes of men, at all times, and under all circumstances."

As *The Belgic Confession* of 1561 ominously reminds its readers, the final chapter of the final book of the Bible can threaten with like solemnity: "If any one takes away from the words of the book of this prophecy, God will take away his share in the tree of life and in the holy city" (Rv 22.19). Elsewhere, too, the New Testament warns: "Take note of those who create dissensions and difficulties, in opposition to the doctrine which you have been taught; avoid them" (Rom 16.17). Therefore, in the words of the first Christian confession to be issued on American soil, *The Cam-*

bridge Platform of 1648, "it is not left in the power of men, officers, churches, or any state in the world to add or diminish or alter anything in the least measure [in Holy Scripture]." Yet it is not only the creedal, confessional, and dogmatic interpretations of Christian Scripture by churches, but also the official interpretations of American Scripture by the justices of the Supreme Court in their normative judgments that can invoke such sanctions, sometimes doing so, moreover, in the vocabulary of doctrinal anathema. Thus Supreme Court Justice Samuel Chase at the end of the eighteenth century defined: "To maintain that our federal, or state legislature possesses such power, if they had not been expressly restrained; would, in my opinion, be a political *heresy,* altogether inadmissible in our free republican governments." And Justice David Davis in the middle of the nineteenth century declared, in continuation of the words quoted earlier from him: "No *doctrine,* involving more pernicious consequences, was ever invented by the wit of man than that any of [the Constitution's] provisions can be suspended during any of the great exigencies of government."

All of this means that from the first there have had to be interpretations of both of these texts—learned and earnest, but sometimes also, as has repeatedly been recognized in both traditions, "tortured construction," or excessively "strict and literal" interpretation, or "strained, confused, and obscure subtleties," or "narrow and artificial," or "elusive at best." For biblical exegesis, the technical term "to interpret" in various languages (including English) can mean either "to translate" or "to expound," also because translation necessarily involves interpretation. For constitutional interpretation, too, the situation may sometimes be obscured by the technical vocabulary of legal hermeneutics. Rather than "to interpret," the technical term used in the language of the Supreme Court during the nineteenth century (and even beyond) is often the grammatical term "to construe," for which the cognate noun is "construction"; therefore the subtitle of Francis Lieber's nineteenth-century *Legal and Political Hermeneutics* is: "Principles of Interpretation and Construction." When the phrase "the construction of the Constitution" appears in a Supreme Court opinion such as that of Chief Justice Roger Brooke Taney in 1837 or in other opinions, therefore, this refers, not, as modern use of the term "construction" might superficially suggest, to how the Constitution of the United States was assembled or composed (for which the usual verb now is "to frame," hence "the framers"), but to how it has been and is being interpreted.

Christian Scripture

"Bible" is taken here to refer to the Christian canon of the Bible, comprising the Old Testament and the New Testament—howsoever one or another church may have defined the exact boundaries of the Old Testament canon. For Christianity inherited from Judaism two libraries of sacred books: one that was preserved in Hebrew and that is traditionally thought to have been fixed by a Jewish synod at Jamnia in about 100 C.E., perhaps in partial reaction to the rise of the church, containing the books that were eventually enumerated in several Protestant Reformed confessions as the authentic canon; the other, preserved in the Greek of the Septuagint translation and carried over into the Latin Vulgate, containing several additional books, which would be dismissed by those same Protestant confessions on the grounds that "the books commonly called Apocrypha, not being of divine inspiration, are no part of the canon of the Scripture; and therefore are of no authority in the church of God, nor to be any otherwise approved, or made use of, than other human writings." In reaction to this Protestant dismissal of the larger canon and the authorization of the narrower canon, the Council of Trent at its fourth session "decided that a written list of the sacred books should be included in this decree in case a doubt should occur to anyone as to which are the books which are accepted by this council"; and it anathematized anyone who "should not accept as sacred and canonical these entire books and all their parts as they have, by established custom, been read in the Catholic Church, and as contained in the old Latin Vulgate edition." The question of canonicity was complicated by the authority not only of this "old Latin Vulgate edition," but especially of the Greek Septuagint, which included the Apocrypha; for this was the version of the Old Testament quoted most of the time by the evangelists and apostles who composed the New Testament. Once the fierce debates of the Constitutional Congress were settled, the canon of the Constitution, by contrast, was accepted immediately upon its issuance and has continued to be universally normative.

On the surface, a major difference between the two codes would seem to be the possibility of amending the Constitution: no decision of a church council, no creed, no papal definition, no canon law could imaginably put itself forward as an "amendment" to Holy Scripture—although they have in fact functioned as what John Henry Newman in his *Essay on the Development of Christian Doctrine* called "preservative additions," among which, "greater perhaps than any before or since," was the action of the Council of Ephesus in 431 conferring on the Virgin Mary the title of Theotokos, Mother of God. But on closer examination there are, perhaps surprisingly, some similarities between the relation of the original Scripture (that is, the Old Testament) to the New and the relation of the original Constitution to the Bill of Rights. Both the words "New Testament" [*kainē diathēkē,* which could almost be rendered "renewed covenant"] and the word "amend-

ment" here connote continuity as well as change, a change that
is perceived as clarifying, carrying out, making explicit, supple-
menting, and fulfilling the existing code, but not as annulling its
fundamental spirit; it is equally unimaginable that an amendment
to the Constitution could read: "The Constitution of the United
States is hereby abolished and declared null and void." As the
Constitution itself prescribes, a constitutional amendment "shall
be valid to all intents and purposes, *as part of this constitution*"
(art. 5). In the Sermon on the Mount, Jesus draws the contrast
between what "you have heard that it was said to the men of
old" and what "I say to you" (Mt 5.21–22), but he does so only
after having pronounced the stern warning: "Think not that I
have come to abolish the law and the prophets; I have come not
to abolish them but to fulfill them" (Mt 5.17). Therefore the Gospels and the other books of the New Testament, like the amendments to the Constitution, became "valid to all intents and purposes, as part of this" Scripture, which until then had consisted
only of the Old Testament. Some further explanation of this term
"Old Testament" may, consequently, be called for here as well.
Valid though many of the concerns are that have animated the
recent adoption of the term "Hebrew Bible" as the politically
(and even theologically) correct substitute for "Old Testament,"
in order to avoid the idea that the divine covenant with the people of Israel has been superseded by the coming of the gospel — an
idea that the words of Jesus in the Sermon on the Mount just
quoted (Mt 5.17) and the epistles of Paul (Rom 9–11) and, on
that basis, recent confessional statements repudiate — it does not
really fit here. For during most of the history of the church,
"Christian Scripture" has meant the *Greek* Bible, the Septuagint
Old Testament as well as the Greek New Testament, or the Vulgate *Latin* Bible, but decidedly not the *Hebrew* Bible. Therefore
"Old Testament" continues to be its title here.

Although both the Bible and the Constitution are the objects of respect and even of reverence, there is, above all, this fundamental difference between them: the Bible is meant to be prayed and believed, and only therefore acted upon. This is so because the church defines itself by its liturgy: *lex orandi lex credendi,* "the rule of prayer is the rule of faith." As the trial court, quoted by the Supreme Court in *Abington School District* v. *Schempp* (1963), had explained, "the reading of the verses [from the Bible], even without comment, possesses a devotional and religious character and constitutes in effect a religious observance"; and the Supreme Court "agree[d] with the trial court's finding that such an opening exercise is a religious ceremony." And yet, as was noted earlier, the Court had to acknowledge in the same case that "the sessions of this Court are declared open by the crier in a short ceremony, the final phrase of which invokes the grace of God."

Constitutions and the Other "Peoples of the Book"

Although the title "people of the Book" originated as the designation in the Qur'an for Judaism and Christianity, it has become a convenient way of referring to all three of the monotheistic religions that claim descent from Abraham and that accept the authority of a historical revelation set down in a sacred book. In all three religions, therefore, there is as well a special relation between that sacred book as written revelation and the idea of a written constitution, also by contrast with cultures that do not possess either one even though they may have an unwritten "constitution."

If space — and, above all, scholarly competence — permitted (which they do not), juxtaposing "Torah and Constitution" would have a special attraction, also because *Torah* does mean "law" in a way that *Gospel* does not, in spite of the occasional use of such a term as "the law of Christ" to identify it. During many centuries of Jewish history, as the historical books of the Old Testament describe it, the written authority of the Torah, either in creative interaction with the living authority of the prophets or sometimes in tension with it, ordered not only the religious and the liturgical life of the worshiping community, but the morality, diet, and personal hygiene of individuals (as in the Book of Leviticus) and the public and the political institutions of the entire nation (as in the Book of Deuteronomy). As one of the major Reformation confessions put it, "God was pleased to give to the people of Israel . . . ceremonial laws. . . . To them also, as a body politic, he gave sundry judicial laws"; and other and earlier Reformation confessions in the British Isles insisted: "nor the civil precepts thereof ought of necessity be received in any commonwealth." After the close of the era of the prophets, the rise of the Great Synagogue marked the beginnings of the Pharisaical, and eventually the rabbinical and Talmudic, period of the history of the interpretation of Torah. The methods employed by the rabbinical lawyers and their courts bear many instructive analogies to the interpretations of the Constitution of the United States. Moreover, as is demonstrated by the arguments of the various religious parties in the debates since 1948 over whether Israel is a secular state, it is possible on the basis of Torah and Talmud to construct a formidable body of law that can be used to regulate life in a modern technological society, though often by putting a severe strain on the interpretive methodology—not to mention the strain that it can sometimes put on the society and on individual citizens. Conversely, the possibility of obeying the injunctions of Torah and Talmud in a society where they do not carry the force of constitution has been, and continues to be, a major issue both of observance and of interpretation for the

Judaism of the Diaspora—and for the Islam of the Diaspora as well.

For although again (and to a far greater degree) scholarly competence does not make this possible, a comparative study of "Shari'a and Constitution," or perhaps even of "Shari'a *as* Constitution," would have an even broader contemporary relevance at the beginning of the twenty-first century. Shari'a is not only a system for regulating personal conduct and a moral guide for telling the difference between right and wrong, as Michael A. Cook documents in great detail, but a law intended for an entire society. That becomes visible above all in those Muslim societies in which there is still no operative distinction (with apologies for invoking Christian terminology) between "canon law" and "civil law," or even between "church" and "state," so that, for example, the punishments prescribed by the Qur'an for adultery or theft are, as a matter of course, carried out by the authority of the state and by its courts and police. Thus a late-twentieth-century textbook of Muslim jurisprudence, entitled *Code of Islamic Laws* and published in Lahore, Pakistan, in 1997, can present itself in its subtitle as containing "the criminal and civic laws of Islam directly deduced from the Qur'an." Even in more secularized states that stand within the Muslim tradition, amendments and adjustments are, at most, possible only in the framework of terms dictated by the law of the Holy Book. For example, in the search for equity in the laws governing marriage and divorce and for legal protection against polygamy, legislation that would directly prohibit something that the Qur'an permits is out of the question. Sometimes, therefore, the best recourse is a law, such as the controversial Egyptian "Law 44," allowing a couple to sign a prenuptial agreement, enforceable by the courts as a contract, under which the husband promises not to avail himself of the

Quranic privilege of taking more than one wife. The evolution of the state constitution and of secular law in Turkey during the twentieth century, beginning with the reforms of Mustafa Kemal Atatürk, and the subsequent vicissitudes of that experiment, provide a laboratory for the development of interpretive methods that must be of great interest and importance to interpreters of both sacred and secular "scriptures" in other societies.

In both Judaism and Islam, therefore, these Scriptures, Torah and Qur'an, are—or at any rate can be, and at times have been, and in some places still are—political "law" and even "constitutions" in a way that the New Testament has been within Christendom only in rare experiments. By a rather loose construction of the term "theocracy," John Calvin's Geneva and the cognate but distinct legal systems attempted in Oliver Cromwell's England and in Puritan New England have sometimes been seen as such experiments, as has the Anabaptist community of Münster; even there, however, the Old Testament rather than the New provided the substance of the jurisprudence. But far beyond these relatively brief and relatively isolated instances, the theme of "Christian Scripture and American Scripture," as a comparative study of methods of interpretation, can be especially poignant, important, and instructive.

American Scripture

The term "American Scripture," too, probably requires clarification; for Pauline Maier's widely received book of 1997, *American Scripture,* has employed this term to designate the Declaration of Independence rather than the Constitution. Several possible explanations suggest themselves for such a designation. The word "Scripture" is usually taken to mean a text that not only is the product of divine "inspiration" itself (2 Tm 3.16) but goes on to produce "inspirations" in its readers. Thus it could be argued that not the Constitution but two other texts above all would qualify for this title of "American Scripture": the Declaration of Independence of 1776 and the Gettysburg Address of 1863, as for example they were combined, with each other and with the Constitution, by Justice Douglas, speaking for the Court in 1963, when he cited as his authority "the conception of political equality from the Declaration of Independence, to Lincoln's Gettysburg Address, to the Fifteenth, Seventeenth, and Nineteenth Amendments."

The doctrine of the Declaration of Independence that "governments derive their just powers from the consent of the governed," as it is used both in popular political discourse and in textbooks on civics and American history, does have the standing of an American article of faith, and sometimes is even mistakenly attributed to the Constitution rather than to the Declaration. The triad "life, liberty, and the pursuit of happiness" from the Declaration of Independence replaced the standard formulation of John Locke, although the formulation "life, liberty, or property" did eventually become constitutional, but only with the Fifth Amendment and then again with the Fourteenth Amendment in 1868 (amend. 14, sec. 1). The triad of "life, liberty, and the pursuit of happiness" holds a place in American political rhetoric, and probably in popular consciousness, as though it were *the* Bill of Rights and as though the term "unalienable rights" were in the Constitution rather than in the Declaration; for in the Declaration, as Louis H. Pollak has said, Thomas Jefferson "was elevating commonplace and often awkwardly phrased ideas into the permanent rhetoric of the nation." And several phrases near the beginning and the end of the Declaration of Independence—"endowed by their Creator," "Nature and Nature's God," and "appealing to the Supreme Judge of the world for the rectitude of our intentions"—explicitly posit a theistic basis for the doctrine of "natural rights." Such a basis is conspicuously (perhaps even intentionally) absent from the Constitution, for which the Constitutional Convention was "scolded" by several participants, including especially Benjamin Franklin. Nevertheless, Justice Douglas seemed to be referring to the Constitution, and not only to the Declaration of Independence, when, speaking for the Court, he wrote in 1952 that "we are a religious people whose institutions presuppose a Supreme Being." The Declaration of Independence has, moreover, sometimes been cited as an authority by the Supreme Court—though, admittedly, less often than might be expected—in its interpretation of the Constitution. And, echoing the relative assessment of the two documents by abolitionists like William Lloyd Garrison, one recent interpretation of the controversial opinion rendered by Justice Holmes in the case of *Buck* v. *Bell* (1927) can even fault him on the grounds that "he took the Constitution for his text and rejected the Declaration of Independence."

Similarly, "government of the people, by the people, for the people" from the Gettysburg Address has become the most canonical of all definitions of American democracy; and the Address itself, with its echoes of the Funeral Oration of Pericles, has been memorized by generations of schoolchildren—at least when schoolchildren were still required to memorize anything. Its opening reference to "fourscore and seven years ago" is dated from the Declaration of Independence of 1776, not from the Constitution of 1789, just as the Constitution itself is dated: "the seventeenth day of September, in the year of our Lord one thousand seven hundred and eighty-seven, *and of the Independence of the United States of America the twelfth*" (italics added). It is from the Declaration, not from the Constitution, that the Gettysburg Address quotes, as that to which the "new nation" was dedicated upon being "brought forth" and "conceived in liberty": "the proposition that all men are created equal." The bicentennial of the Constitution after "tenscore years" did provide the occasion for a thoughtful essay in which Justice Thurgood Marshall spoke to the consciences of many when he declared that "while the Union survived the civil war, the Constitution did not. In its place arose a new, more promising basis for justice and equality, the fourteenth amendment, ensuring protection of the life, liberty, and property of *all* persons against deprivations without due process, and guaranteeing equal protection." "I plan," Justice Marshall continued on a personal note, "to celebrate the bicentennial of the Constitution as a living document, including the Bill of Rights and the other amendments protecting individual freedoms and human rights." But consideration of those issues and of "the greater ideals of the American Republic" had already evoked from W. E. B. DuBois, in *The Souls of Black Folk* of 1903, the assertion that "there are to-day no truer exponents of the pure human spirit of the Declaration of Independence than the American Negroes," without so much as a mention of the Constitution or even of the Bill of Rights. Moreover, a comparison between the scale of the national celebrations of the bicentennials of these two "living documents" may serve as a reminder that in a culture in which almost no one keeps namedays but everyone observes birthdays, it is the Declaration of Independence of 1776, not the Constitution of 1789, that Americans celebrate on the Fourth of July as *the* national holiday.

Nevertheless, it still is the Constitution, and not the Declaration of Independence, that functions as the normative American Scripture. During the intense—and continuing—civil rights struggle for equality, political debate and rhetoric have often focused on the formula of the Declaration of Independence, "All men are created equal and are endowed by their Creator with certain unalienable rights." This formula was invoked with moral and oratorical power by Dr. Martin Luther King, Jr., who in his address of August 1963, "I Have a Dream," called this formula the American "creed" and earlier had said of the Declaration of Independence: "Never has a sociopolitical document proclaimed more profoundly and eloquently the sacredness of human personality." In American law, however, as distinct from these dramatic highpoints, it is the Thirteenth and Fourteenth Amendments, and above all the requirement of "the equal protection of the laws" (amend. 14, sec. 1), that has been the subject of controversy over the logic of textual exegesis, and therefore of judicial interpretation in such a decisive Supreme Court case as *Brown* v. *Board of Education* of 1954. And that makes the Constitution the normative "American Scripture" in a sense that the Declaration of Independence is not.

The Interpretive Communities

At work in the interpretation of both texts has been "the power of an interpretive community to constitute the objects upon which its members (also and simultaneously constituted) can then agree." Both for Christian Scripture and for American Scripture, and with some striking parallels between the two, it is possible to identify four chief interpretive communities, which are distinct but which constantly interact with one another:

1. *We the people* in their voting booths and in their pews. It was in their name that the Constitution claimed to be speaking, as its opening words attest. As Justice Joseph Story insisted in 1816, "The constitution of the United States was ordained and established, not by the states in their sovereign capacities, but emphatically, as the preamble of the constitution declares, by 'the People of the United States.' " Even earlier, Justice James Wilson

posed the question, and answered it in the affirmative: "Do the People of the United States form a Nation?" And again: "This tribunal [the Supreme Court], therefore, was erected, and the powers of which we have spoken conferred upon it, not by the Federal Government, *but by the people of the States, who formed and adopted that Government, and conferred upon it all the powers, legislative, executive, and judicial, which it now possesses.*" This implied, Chief Justice Marshall contended, that it would be misguided, and a fundamental distortion of the text, to restrict the Constitution to a learned elite and to read it as "a legal code . . . [that] would, probably, never be understood by the public." The Supreme Court quoted these words of Chief Justice Marshall to good effect a half-century later; and in this aftermath of the Civil War the Supreme Court also reaffirmed that "the Constitution is the fundamental law of the United States. By it the people have created a government, defined its powers, prescribed their limits, distributed them among the different departments, and directed, in general, the manner of their exercise. No department of the government has any other powers than those thus delegated to it by the people." Such statements by the Court could easily be multiplied. Thus the formula of James Madison, as stated in the House of Representatives in 1794, "The censorial power is in the people over the Government, and not in the Government over the people," could be quoted by the Court nearly two centuries later to interpret the First Amendment. Arguing in a similar vein, Justice Felix Frankfurter said in 1927 that because "the Constitution is a *Constitution,* and not merely a detailed code of prophetic restrictions against the ineptitudes and inadequacies of legislators and administrators," it followed that "ultimate protection is to be found in the people themselves, their zeal for liberty, their respect for one another and for the common good." As the source of the government's authority, the people have also retained those rights that they have not explicitly surrendered. A chilling and profoundly more relativistic version of this reliance on "we the people" is reflected in what Grant Gilmore in his Storrs Lecture for 1974 at the Yale Law School called the "single, frightening" axiom of Oliver Wendell Holmes, Jr., written before his elevation to the Supreme Court, that "the first requirement of a sound body of law is that it should correspond with the actual feelings and demands of the community, *right or wrong*." He elaborated on this axiom when he was on the Court, more than a third of a century later, in words that are often quoted:

> When men have realized that time has upset many fighting faiths, they may come to believe even more than they believe the very foundations of their own conduct that the ultimate good desired is better reached by free trade in ideas—that the best test of truth is the power of the thought to get itself accepted in the competition of the market, and that truth is the only ground upon which their wishes safely can be carried out. That at any rate is the theory of our Constitution. It is an experiment, as all life is an experiment.

Bruce A. Ackerman has seen the locus of ongoing interpretation of American Scripture in the cumulative experience of "we the people," as reflected in such decisive events of American history as the Civil War and the New Deal.

For the interpretation of Christian Scripture, the authority of "we the people" could be invoked, in the fourth century and again in modern times, in opposition to the trinitarian orthodoxy of the Council of Nicaea, including the innovation of its use of the term *ousia* [essence or being], and therefore of the Nicene watchword *homoousios,* on the grounds that it "gives offense as being unknown to the people, because it is not contained in the Scriptures . . . [so] that 'essence' be never in any case used of God again." But already in the second century, Irenaeus of Lyons, after reciting the orthodox rule of faith, had appealed to the authority of the people, even though they might be illiterate (or at any rate ignorant of Greek, which, of course, was thought to be tantamount to being illiterate):

> Those who, in the absence of written documents, have believed this faith, are barbarians, so far as regards our language; but as regards doctrine, manner, and tenor of life, they are, because of faith, very wise indeed; and they do please God, ordering their conversation in all righteousness, chastity, and wisdom. If anyone were to preach to these men the inventions of the heretics, speaking to them in their own language, they would at once stop their ears and flee as far off as possible, not enduring even to listen to the blasphemous address.

And at almost the same time it was possible for Origen of Alexandria to appeal to the authority of that on which "the entire church is unanimous," while leaving open many other questions on which its authority had not yet spoken. In the polemics of the schism between the Eastern and the Western church, it became customary to pit the authority of believing "wise citizens" against that of their leaders. Ultimately, the authority of "the people" as the "interpretive community" for Christian Scripture could mean, as the patriarchs and prelates of Eastern Orthodoxy put it in 1848 in their response to Pope Pius IX, that "neither patriarchs nor councils could have introduced novelties amongst us, because *the protector of religion is the very body of the church, even the people themselves,* who desire their religious worship to be ever unchanged and of the same kind as that of their fathers." But at nearly the same time, that authority was also being invoked elsewhere in the opposite direction, against the authority of any creeds whatsoever, and against the ecclesiastical requirement "that none have a right to the communion of the church, but such as . . . are come to a very high degree of doctrinal information"; for "it is not necessary that persons should have a particular knowledge or distinct apprehension of all divinely revealed truths in order to entitle them to a place in the church." Always implicit, and sometimes explicit, in these references to "the people" of the church has been the assumption that because "no one can attain the true faith unless he hears the word of God," it is necessary not only to "read the Gospels and other Scriptures in church" but to "interpret them to the people."

The parallel between the constitutional and the biblical "we the people" comes into view in the two related phrases that are often used for them: "the consent of the governed" and *consensus fidelium*. For the Declaration of Independence, this is the fourth of the five truths held to be self-evident, after equality and other rights but before the right of revolution, "that, to secure these rights, governments are instituted among men, *deriving their just powers from the consent of the governed*"; the opening phrase of the preamble of the Constitution, "we the people," has often been seen as embodying and expressing this "consent of the governed." The Latin phrase *consensus fidelium,* which achieved theological currency well before the campaign to make decision-making in the church more "democratic," can claim support from all three major confessional traditions: Protestant, Eastern Orthodox, and Roman Catholic. It expresses, for example, the claim of one Reformation confession to represent the *magnus consensus* of "our churches," as well as its requirement for church unity of a *consen-*

tire de doctrina evangelii; it is epitomized in the Eastern Orthodox teaching just quoted, that "the protector of religion is the very body of the church, even *the people themselves*"; and it received its classic modern formulation in the essay "On Consulting the Faithful in Matters of Doctrine," which John Henry Newman published in *The Rambler* in 1858. In an atmosphere that was about to produce the *Syllabus of Errors* of Pope Pius IX in 1864 and the decree of the First Vatican Council on the infallibility of the pope in 1869/1870, this definition by a recent convert of the role of the laity as bearers of authentic Catholic tradition, which went well beyond the standard appeal to "the universal consent of the fathers," aroused widespread suspicion, of which Newman was not cleared until 1867. (He was named cardinal by Pope Leo XIII in 1879.) The *consensus fidelium,* and in considerable measure Newman's understanding of it, achieved official vindication when the Second Vatican Council issued its *Decree on the Apostolate of the Laity* at its eighth session, on 18 November 1965.

2. *The academic scholars* of the professoriat with their historical research and their footnotes, who are a learned and often quarrelsome lot. Both documents have generated a scholarly tradition, without which it is no longer possible to interpret them. Thus Richard A. Posner suggests: "The real significance of constitutional theory is, I believe, as a sign of the increased academification of law school professors, who are much more inclined than they used to be to write for other professors rather than for judges and practitioners." The study of both texts has been shaped by the historical scholarship of the nineteenth and twentieth centuries, which has produced entire libraries of erudite monographs, learned journals, reference works, and textbooks about each of them (of which the many works cited in the Bibliography to this book are only a sample). It has also sometimes

produced, as David Rabban termed it, "the chasm . . . between the world of legal scholarship and the judiciary," a chasm that can be at least as wide in the church.

For, even more than the Constitution, the Bible, as a text written long ago and far away in Hebrew and in Greek, requires esoteric learning for its scholarly interpretation. The twin emphases of the Protestant Reformation on biblical authority and on the universal priesthood of all believers necessarily implied not only that technical theological terms "should not be employed in sermons delivered to common, unlearned people, but simple folk should be spared them," but also the converse, that "those things which are necessary to be known, believed, and observed for salvation, are so clearly propounded and opened in some place of Scripture or other, that *not only the learned, but the unlearned,* in a due use of the ordinary means, may attain unto a sufficient understanding of them." In practice, however, the fullest possible "understanding of them" and the defense of that "understanding" against its adversaries depended on scholars. Therefore Henry VIII explained that he had "caused our bishops, and other the most discreet and *best learned men of our clergy* of this our whole realm, to be assembled in our convocation, for the full debatement and quiet determination" of "diversity in opinions . . . as well concerning certain articles necessary to our salvation"; it was these "best learned men of our clergy" who produced the several sets of sixteenth-century Anglican articles of religion, from *The Ten Articles* of 1536 to *The Thirty-Nine Articles* of 1571. Even the Baptists and Anabaptists, who frequently tended to disparage academic theology because in the interpretation of Scripture it overemphasized learning at the expense of the inner testimony of the Holy Spirit, could nevertheless express concern about "innocent *and unlearned* persons." Therefore it was from that branch of Protestantism that there came one of the most explicit recogni-

tions "that such as God hath given gifts to interpret the Scriptures, tried in the exercise of prophecy, *giving attendance to study
and learning,* may and ought by the appointment of the congregation to teach publicly the word." But this was accompanied by
the warning that their being "excellent, great, or learned" did not
exempt them from the discipline of the local congregation. Yet
the contrary Catholic and Orthodox doctrine of authority, as re-
stated in the nineteenth century, that not Scripture alone but
"genuine tradition, i.e., the unbroken transmission, partly oral,
partly by writing, of the doctrine delivered by Jesus Christ and
the apostles, is an authoritative source of teaching for all successive generations of Christians" could make theological learning
even more important; for "this tradition is partly to be found in
the consensus of the great ecclesiastical bodies, standing in historical continuity with the primitive church, *partly is to be gathered
by a scientific [wissenschaftlich] method from the written documents of
all centuries.*" Again in the twentieth century, the challenges of
ecumenism were said to have special pertinence not only for "ordinary Christian life" but also for "theological and historical research." But the end result of such an "academification" could be,
and sometimes was, the emergence of two normative theologies:
"the one, that which is contained in the confessions; the other,
that which found its most fitting expression in the theology of
the professors of the nineteenth century."

3. *The professional and certified practitioners* with their briefs
and their sermons, in their service to their clients for the day-to-
day application of the text to the situations of human life. In
Christian preaching, beginning supremely with the preaching of
Jesus himself as in the Sermon on the Mount and then in interpretations of it, persuading the hearer by these professionals has
always entailed using Scripture to present "the character of the
speaker," *ēthos,* to form a bond with "the frame of mind of the

audience," *pathos,* and to enhance "the structure of the argument," *logos.* The same three components, as they are formulated in Aristotle's *Rhetoric,* pertain to the function of the lawyer when addressing a judge or a jury as barrister. Although there has always been wide room for a fanciful, almost playful, element in the figurative and allegorical interpretation of the Bible, it remains essential to the practice of biblical preaching that it be credible in its use of the sacred text. This means, even for the devotees of allegorical exegesis, that the *sensus literalis* remains primary. Yet Christian Scripture is not only the supreme epic and the inexhaustible source of poetic figures or literary allusions and the most fruitful of all texts for thousands of musical compositions (all of which it is) but the Great Code. This designation involves code as codification, code as supreme law, code as guide for conduct, code as cryptogram, code as genetic code, code as *codex,* "codes and codas." To that extent it shares with any other code, whether it be the Code of Hammurabi or the Code of Justinian or the Code of Napoleon or the Code of Canon Law (or the Constitution), the need to be interpreted in a manner that those outside the charmed circle of interpreters will not find arbitrary, even if they disagree with it or cannot always follow its reasoning. Conversely, when the use of Scripture moves from "sermon" to "summa," the argument of the biblical interpreter must be able to convince, not only to persuade; so it is as well with the interpreter of the Constitution.

4. *The hierarchy* with their robes and their decrees — and they can trump all the others; for "the teaching authority to hold forth on any ecclesiastical subjects . . . is granted only to bishops by the grace from above," and, in an oft-quoted epigram, the Supreme Court is not final because it is infallible, but infallible because it is final. Therefore it is not an exaggeration to speak of "the cult of the courts." The English word "hierarchy" can be used in at

least two ways, as these are defined in the *Oxford English Dictionary:* for "the collective body of ecclesiastical rulers" in various churches and denominations, who are charged with setting down the normative interpretation of Christian Scripture by legislating, as the Council of Ephesus of 431 did about the First Council of Nicaea of 325, that "all those who have a clear and blameless faith will understand, *interpret,* and proclaim it in this way"; and then more broadly for any "body of persons . . . ranked in grade," therefore for the justices of the "one supreme court" (art. 3, sec. 1) of the United States, who are charged with setting down the normative interpretation of American Scripture.

At the outset it is essential to recognize the differences and the similarities between these two hierarchies, for example in the important principle that American jurisprudence calls "the separation of powers," classically defined by Justice Louis Dembits Brandeis: "The doctrine of the separation of powers was adopted by the Convention of 1787, not to promote efficiency but to preclude the exercise of arbitrary power. The purpose was, not to avoid friction, but, by means of the inevitable friction incident to the distribution of the governmental powers among three departments, to save the people from autocracy." Under the Constitution of the United States, the judicial branch stands alongside the legislative and the executive branches, and much of the history of the Supreme Court has been taken up with defining the boundaries separating it from the other two branches. But a Christian bishop is, at any rate traditionally, not only preacher and teacher and celebrant of the sacred mysteries, but judge, lawgiver, and executive, all at the same time; this applies *a fortiori* to the collective body of bishops, especially when they are assembled in a church council, particularly a council that lays claim to the title "ecumenical." In that sense, therefore, the doctrine of "distribution of powers" does not apply; nevertheless, something very much like this doctrine has been at work in the debates over the relation between such a council and the authority of the bishop of Rome.

But the two hierarchies do have in common the serious responsibility, in words of Justice Frankfurter that could have been spoken about either one, not to "draw on our merely personal and private notions and disregard the limits that bind judges in their judicial function," but to "lay aside private views in discharging their judicial functions. This is achieved through training, professional habits, self-discipline, and that fortunate alchemy by which men are loyal to the obligation with which they are entrusted." Where that did not suffice and where there was therefore some "ground for believing that such unconscious feelings may operate in the ultimate judgment, or may not unfairly lead others to believe they are operating, judges recuse themselves," as Justice Frankfurter himself did in this particular case of *Public Utilities Commission* v. *Pollak*. In the early days of the Court, Associate Justice William Paterson, citing the debates of the Constitutional Congress in which he himself had participated, subordinated his own moral and philosophical position to the intended meaning of the Constitution as he remembered it to have been. On similar grounds, *The Barmen Declaration* of 1934 by the Evangelical Church of Germany, in protest against the Nazi effort to corrupt the church's confession, rejected "the false doctrine as though the church were permitted to abandon the form of its message and order *to its own pleasure* or to changes in prevailing ideological and political convictions. . . . in the service of any arbitrarily chosen desires, purposes, and plans." In many circles, however, it has come to be regarded as sophisticated to dismiss this approach, skeptically or even cynically, as naive or disingenuous, as window dressing for the *real* motives of both bishops and justices, which are class or power, pride or prejudice.

Nevertheless, it has characterized much of the behavior of many justices and bishops much of the time—including the often observed phenomenon, for which Justice Frankfurter himself and Pope John XXIII are sometimes cited as examples, that their previous attitudes and "private views" are not an accurate predictor of what their official decisions will be once they have assumed their supreme office.

This book is, consequently, a review not primarily of private or scholarly interpretations either of Christian Scripture, by professors of exegesis or individual believers, or of American Scripture, by constitutional lawyers or individual citizens, though all of these are, of course, often involved in it. It is a history neither of theology nor of political philosophy, much less a comparison between the two, nor a history of relations between church and state, but a history of the "constructions" that have been promulgated by those who bear official responsibility for binding interpretation: the official councils, creeds, confessions, and public liturgies of the Christian tradition for the interpretation of Christian Scripture; and their counterpart in the interpretation of American Scripture, the decisions and opinions of the secular American equivalent of the ecumenical council, the Supreme Court. For although the Supreme Court of the United States does not, of course, refer to itself as an ecumenical council and would be prohibited from doing so by the First Amendment, church councils have repeatedly identified themselves as a supreme court—sometimes as supreme even over the papacy.

Text and Context

It is probably necessary also to "stipulate" (to use a lawyerly word) that this effort to engage in a style of "intellectual history that takes serious ideas seriously, as ideas, rather than as instru-

ments of production and consumption," and therefore to con-
centrate on the history of the interpretation of the two normative
texts, does not in any way "personify ideas in themselves and
regard them as self-standing agencies in history," as though political, social, cultural, and psychological factors did not profoundly affect how justices read the Constitution or how confes-
sors read the Bible. Of course they do, and they always have.
Beneath every robe, be it judicial or clerical (or even academic),
there beats a human heart. In the eloquent reminder of 1960
(some of whose details would need to be revised somewhat) by
my sometime colleague Karl Nickerson Llewellyn, who was, as
Grant Gilmore said of him, "flamboyant both in his personality
and his prose style," as this passage illustrates,

> Judges are human, all of them. They are, moreover,
> all American and almost all male, almost all of at least
> middle age, all readers of news, most of them affected—
> though with divergence in their "law"-conditioned resis-
> tances—by those tides of interest and of opinion which
> wash over the decades, the years, sometimes shorter pe-
> riods. . . . They are almost all white-collar in back-
> ground, and raised in Judaeo-Christian morality. . . . It is
> an almost sure bet that there are not two single-taxers,
> polygamists, anarchists, spies, Moslems, ex-convicts, ma-
> jor poets, first-class trombones, or mining engineers
> among the lot.

With only a few appropriate adjustments, Llewellyn's description
would fit churchmen as well. Ingrained prejudice, mixed moti-
vation, and the tendency to make the worse appear the better
reason are part of the moral ambiguity that flesh is heir to, an
ambiguity to which neither bishops nor justices (nor scholars)

are immune. The persistence of the phenomenon that a confession issued jointly by Catholics and Orthodox in 1993 calls "the interference of extra-ecclesial interests," as well as the interference of extra-constitutional considerations, would have to be an important part of any total narrative. But that does not justify reducing the textual and doctrinal debates to a mere rationalization. An "unease" with the simplistic "political interpretation" of such Supreme Court decisions as *Brown* and *Griswold,* Bruce Ackerman has therefore persuasively urged, "will, I hope, motivate you to consider the alternative with a new seriousness: Can/should we understand *Brown* and *Griswold* as valid—indeed profound—acts of constitutional *interpretation?*" As he himself points out, the same question would apply to the New Deal. It could even apply to the *Dred Scott* decision. Similarly, the twelve-hundredth anniversary of the restoration of icons by the Seventh Ecumenical Council, the Second Council of Nicaea in 787, prompted this methodological reflection:

> At the very least, if doctrine did not determine the grand strategy of the opposing forces in this battle, it did provide most of the ammunition on both sides. The history of warfare would not make sense without the history of ordnance, nor would the history of politics without the history of political rhetoric. Therefore it behooves even a modern historian, in interpreting this chapter in the political history of art, to look beyond the politics to the rhetoric, including the theological rhetoric. Byzantium was famous for its weaponry, especially for "Greek fire," a secret chemical formula for its most frightening naval armament. It was no less famous for its theological weaponry. This is a study of the Byzantine theological arsenal.

Both the interpretation of the Constitution as American Scripture and the interpretation of the Bible as Christian Scripture are certainly a great deal more than parsing the grammar and probing the vocabulary of an authoritative text—but they must never be less! On this insistence, those who are often labeled "textualists" in their interpretive philosophy and those who could therefore not inappropriately be labeled "*con*textualists" would, or should, agree. In one sense, therefore, the question of this book is very narrow: What are the means and methods by which official interpreters read their normative texts? But given the massive authority of those texts, as well as the magisterial standing of those authorities, this narrow question is also a decisive question, and one that can be extremely broad in its implications.

"Binocular Vision"

Jurisprudence and Christian confession have had a long and checkered historical symbiosis. *The Theodosian Code* made the confession of the Trinity a legal requirement; and the author of one of the most carefully wrought confessions in the controversies over the relation between the divine and the human nature in Christ, as well as of a christological confession that is sung alongside *The Niceno-Constantinopolitan Creed* in the Eastern Orthodox liturgy, was the same Emperor Justinian who codified the Roman law. Especially in recent times, scholarship in the history of law has been making a major contribution to the study of theology. The works of David Daube, Harold J. Berman, and John T. Noonan are outstanding examples, among many others, of such a contribution. More recently, and with a generous acknowledgment of my concept of "binocular vision," the historian of law John Witte, Jr., has launched a four-volume examination of the legal doctrines in each of the major traditions coming out of the Protestant Reformation.

Together with other recent books, this is, then, an effort at a measure of scholarly reciprocity, what Aristotle in the *Nicomachean Ethics* calls an *antidōrea,* a gift in return. Although it seeks to be informed by the best and most recent scholarship, it cites no sitting justices or sitting bishops or pending cases, and is not intended as a direct intervention in the fray of the current exegetical debates, whether biblical or constitutional. But it does attempt to contribute indirectly to these debates, in the hope that the study of the twenty centuries of interpreting Christian Scripture, out of which it comes, may be of some help and illumination also to those who stand in the tradition of the two centuries of interpreting American Scripture.

Cruxes of Interpretation in the Bible and in the Constitution

How can I understand unless some one gives me the clue?
(Acts 8.31 NEB)

Interpretive Imperatives

Christian exegetes of Holy Scripture have often spoken of a passage as a *crux interpretum,* a crux of the interpreters and of interpretation, defined as "a difficulty which it torments or troubles one greatly to interpret or explain." It may be this because it contains words that are difficult or impossible to understand: even after so many centuries of New Testament scholarship, the Revised Standard Version, having rendered the statement of the Sermon on the Mount as "Whoever *insults* his brother shall be liable to the council" (Mt 5.22), is obliged to explain the translation "insults" in a footnote: "Greek 'says Raca to' (an obscure term of abuse)." Or it may be a *crux interpretum* because the passage raises seemingly insuperable doctrinal difficulties: in the light of the confession of *The Niceno-Constantinopolitan Creed*, re-cited every day at mass, that Christ the Son of God is *homoousios*, "consubstantial, one in being with the Father," orthodox inter-preters of all denominations throughout Christian history have had to ask what it could possibly mean that on the cross, quoting Psalm 22.1, "about the ninth hour Jesus cried with a loud voice, 'Eloi, Eloi, láma sabach-thani?' that is, 'My God, my God, why hast thou forsaken me?' " (Mt 27.46). Among many other *cruces interpretum* in the Constitution is what Sanford Levinson calls "the embarrassing Second Amendment": "A well regulated Mi-litia, being necessary to the security of a free State, the right of the people to keep and bear Arms, shall not be infringed" (amend. 2). After the probing of the grammar of its unique pre-amble, or the examination of what *militia* meant in English law, or the alleged combing of last wills and testaments to count the number of individual citizens in the colonial period who "kept and bore arms," the amendment would still seem to be, as the translators of the RSV admitted about the Aramaic word *Raca* in the Sermon on the Mount, "obscure." Even beyond its tech-nical meaning, therefore, *cruces interpretum*, "cruxes of interpre-tation," is a fitting term for the issues and ambiguities of inter-pretation that are faced by the exegetes both of Christian and of American Scripture.

"You are called upon to deliberate on [the] . . . Constitu-tion." "Search the Scriptures; for in them ye think ye have eternal life: and they are they which testify of me" (Jn 5.39 AV). These two imperatives, the first from the opening sentence of the first of the *Federalist Papers* and the second from the sayings of Jesus in the New Testament according to the Authorized ("King James") Version, would seem, on their face, to be straightforward enough in support of the imperative of interpreting the norma-tive text—and of getting it right. It is an imperative that the several interpretive communities in both traditions, as these communities have been identified in the preceding chapter, have long taken with utmost seriousness as the mission statement that validates their very existence.

On closer historical and grammatical examination, however, both imperatives prove to be considerably more complicated. The full sentence with which *The Federalist* opens reads: "After an unequivocal experience of the inefficacy of the subsisting Federal Government, you are called upon to deliberate on a new Constitution for the United States of America." The readers from the former colony of New York, which was now a state, for whom *The Federalist* was originally intended, were being "called upon" (that is, not merely invited to an academic and intellectual exercise, but summoned to an official political responsibility) to "deliberate on" (that is, not simply to ponder, study, or do research, but to examine with a view toward taking official political action) a Constitution for the United States of America that was "new" (that is, not yet ratified, but still at the stage of being proposed and debated in the several former British colonies). They were expected to do this, moreover, "after an unequivocal experience of the inefficacy of the subsisting [existing] Federal Government," not only an "unequivocal" but "a disappointing experience," as it had been attempted under the Articles of Confederation; the Articles had been adopted by the Second Continental Congress in November 1777 and ratified in 1781, but were now to be superseded by the ratification of the new Constitution. And the title "the United States of America" — whether this title was to be construed with a singular or with a plural verb, both constructions being employed at that time, although the singular has now become standard — appears as the designation for an existing political entity, even though the document that everyone now calls "*the* Constitution of the United States" was not yet in force.

That was the full context of the exhortation "You are called upon to deliberate on . . . [the] Constitution."

Especially since the Protestant Reformation, with its emphasis on the sole authority of Scripture, Jesus' words "Search the Scriptures" have been construed by creeds and confessions of the churches as an imperative, in their citation of this text but above all in their total practice. *The Westminster Confession of Faith* of 1647, buttressed by, as its subtitle says, the "Quotations and Texts of Scripture Annexed," is explicitly quoting the words of this verse as a commandment of Christ when it argues that all Christian believers, not merely the officials of the Roman Catholic Church (or of any other church, including its own Presbyterian Church), possess "the right unto, and interest in the Scriptures, and are commanded, in the fear of God, to read *and search them*"; and its authors faithfully, indeed exhaustively, obeyed the command of this verse by searching the Scriptures and then producing more than fifteen hundred such scriptural proof texts for its several doctrines. Other confessions, too, including even some that coordinate Scripture and tradition in their doctrine of authority, take pains to search out biblical proof texts. At the same time, an Eastern Orthodox confession of the seventeenth century, written in Greek, could quote the Greek verb *ereunate* [search] from this verse, in opposition to the universally Protestant doctrine of the "perspicuity of Scripture," to prove the exact opposite, namely, that "if Divine Scripture were clear to all Christians who read it, the Lord would not have commanded those who desire to obtain salvation to *search* it."

But further "searching" and researching—to begin with the grammar—has suggested that this passage from the Gospels may not be an imperative at all. As it stands, the Greek verb *ereunate* could be an imperative, as it was translated in the Authorized Version, as well as already in the Latin Vulgate ("Scrutamini

Scripturas"), in Luther's German Bible ("Suchet in der Schrift"), and in many other versions. Nevertheless, in the immediate context of this discourse of Jesus in the fifth chapter of the Gospel of John, a fairly strong case can be made for its being an indicative instead. For Jesus is addressing opponents who already "think they have eternal life" in the Scriptures and who already therefore are incessantly searching (or even "ransacking") them — and who therefore certainly need no command from him to go on doing that. He would appear to be saying instead that what they do need is the right clue, which, it can be asserted without serious exaggeration, is not to be found through still further searching of the Scriptures as such, but through finally looking up from the sacred page to the face of the One to whom those Scriptures bear testimony. Far from being the command that the Authorized Version takes it to be, then, it may well be an indicative — and, moreover, an indicative with at least some negative connotation, for so pedantically attending to the *logoi,* or words of God, while failing to recognize the Word of God, the *Logos,* now that he has come to them in the flesh (Jn 1.1–14). In the one other instance of this Greek verb in the Gospel of John the negative connotation is even more explicit; for there the Pharisees urge Nicodemus: "*Search* and you will see that no prophet is to rise from Galilee" (Jn 7.52). The Revised Standard Version, in an equivocation that may have been intentional, evades the problem by translating the words of Jesus as "You search," which does sound like an indicative but might possibly be an imperative; and the New English Bible has "You study the scriptures diligently." Thus, in an irony that has many parallels throughout the history of biblical interpretation, the most frequently quoted command to interpret the Bible must be seen as itself a crux in biblical interpretation.

"Unless Someone Will Give Me the Clue"

As a fifth-century confession reminded its readers, Christ after the resurrection "would go in among his disciples . . . and open up the secrets of the Holy Scriptures after enlightening their understanding." Therefore, in the first recorded communication of the resurrected Christ to his disciples, as reported in the Gospel of Luke, "beginning with Moses and all the prophets, he interpreted to them in all the Scriptures the things concerning himself" (Lk 24.27). The elaboration of that interpretive method and the identification of its limitations would be a major preoccupation for later generations. The Book of Acts, which is a continuation of the narrative of the Gospel of Luke (Acts 1.1–3), describes an encounter between the apostle Philip and an Ethiopian eunuch, who was a minister of the Candace, queen of Ethiopia. He was reading the Book of Isaiah, at the fifty-third chapter, apparently in the Greek translation of the Septuagint. To Philip's question, "Do you understand what you are reading?" the Ethiopian replies, in rabbinical fashion, with another question: "How can I understand unless someone will give me the clue?" (Acts 8.26–39 NEB).

The answer to those questions, in turn, has characteristically proceeded on several levels. One solution to the problem "Do you understand what you are reading?" would have to be grammatical and linguistic, as this has engaged Christian pedagogy (as well as Greco-Roman and Jewish pedagogy before it) since the catechetical school of Alexandria in the second and third centuries: understanding the "meaning" of the individual vocables in the text and the connection between them as expressed in their grammatical relation. But here in the Book of Acts the issue is not philology but prophecy; for the Ethiopian asks the next question (Acts 8.34 NEB): "Now tell me, please, who is it that the prophet is speaking about here: himself or someone else?" Philip proceeds, "starting from this passage" of the Suffering Servant in Isaiah 53, written several centuries earlier, to tell him "the good news of Jesus," who had lived only a few years earlier, as the one of whom Isaiah had prophesied. The events of the life, death, and resurrection of Jesus are "the good news," and therefore "the clue" in the light of which the ancient text that the Ethiopian is "reading" must be "understood." Both the interpretive precedent of Christ after the resurrection and this apostolic obedience to that interpretive precedent established the retrospective herme-neutics by which later history was seen as providing the correct understanding of earlier prophetic Scripture. And when, in turn, Jesus was represented as prophesying that "all this will come upon this generation" (Mt 23.36), or when his apostles prophe-sied "that in the last days there will come times of stress" (2 Tm 3.1) and even produced an entire apocalypse that, after some in-itial difficulty, became part of the canonical New Testament, this New Testament precedent of interpreting prophecy in the light of subsequent history was the foundation for the ongoing exe-getical task. It required considerably less specificity to move from this belief in prophecy-and-fulfillment to the method of interpre-tation by which later events were seen not as fulfillments in the strict sense of the word but as particular *exempla* illustrating a general biblical promise or warning.

Interpretation as a *Crux Interpretum:* "The Thickness of Legal Meaning"

Not only are there, however, many such individual problems of interpretation in both the Bible and the Constitution, but the need or utility of interpretation can itself be a *crux interpretum,* for a number of reasons, including what Robert Cover calls "the thickness of legal meaning." In a provocative taxonomy, which has had its counterpart in nineteenth- and twentieth-century biblical hermeneutics, John Hart Ely distinguished between "interpretivist" methods of arguing from the Constitution on the basis of its history and text and "noninterpretivist" methods on the basis of philosophical and moral doctrines, and he moved from that distinction to argue for "the impossibility of a clause-bound interpretivism." At least superficially, on the basis of their own statements, the confessions of the Protestant Reformation may sometimes be read as claiming that they are replacing the interpretation of Scripture with the simple sense of an uninterpreted *sola Scriptura*. Already in the first article of the first Protestant confession there is this antithesis: "All who say that the gospel is nothing without the approbation [and interpretation] of the church err and slander God." According to *The Scots Confession* of 1560, authority in the church is "neither antiquity [of interpretations, creeds, or doctrines], usurped title [of bishops], lineal [allegedly apostolic] succession [of episcopal ordination], appointed place [Rome or Constantinople or Jerusalem — or Edinburgh], nor the numbers of men approving an error [in a supposedly ecumenical church council or even in a Protestant synod]," but "the true preaching of the word of God [without human glosses or errors]." The implication of this is clear:

> The interpretation of Scripture, we confess, does not belong to any private or public person, nor yet to any kirk for preeminence or precedence, personal or local, which it has above others, but pertains to the Spirit of God by whom the Scriptures were written. When controversy arises about the right understanding of any passage or sentence of Scripture, or for the reformation of any abuse within the kirk of God, we ought not so much

to ask what men have said or done before us, as what the Holy Ghost uniformly speaks within the body of the Scriptures and what Christ Jesus himself did and commanded. For it is agreed by all that the Spirit of God, who is the Spirit of unity, cannot contradict himself. So if the interpretation or opinion of any theologian, kirk, or council, is contrary to the plain word of God written in any other passage of Scripture, it is most certain that this is not the true understanding and meaning of the Holy Ghost, although councils, realms, and nations have approved and received it. *We dare not receive or admit any interpretation which is contrary to any principal point of our faith, or to any other plain text of Scripture, or to the rule of love.*

Six years later, *The Second Helvetic Confession* set forth an even more comprehensive version of *sola Scriptura* in opposition to official "interpretation" of Scripture by the authority of the church: "We hold that interpretation of the Scriptures to be orthodox and genuine which is gleaned from the Scriptures themselves [1] from the nature of the language in which they were written, [2] likewise according to the circumstances in which they were set down, and [3] expounded in the light of like and unlike passages and of many and clearer passages and [4] which agrees with the rule of faith and love, and [5] contributes much to the glory of God and man's salvation." But the suspicions about "interpretation" lingered, as a corollary of the insistence on *sola Scriptura* or sometimes as a corollary of the insistence on the inner illumination by the Holy Spirit, without which "it is impossible that I should entirely understand the Scripture." The Quaker tradition has been obliged to cope with these ambiguities in a special way. In one of its most important nineteenth-century confessional statements, therefore, the Society of Friends reaffirmed this reliance on "the great Inspirer of Scripture [as] ever its true Interpreter," but qualified it with the firm proviso that "whatsoever any one says or does contrary to the Scriptures, though under profession of the immediate guidance of the Holy Spirit, must be reckoned and accounted a mere delusion."

In opposition to this Protestant insistence on the subjectivity of private interpretation and on *sola Scriptura,* the fourth session of the Council of Trent forbade the wrong interpretation and declared the right interpretation normative:

> No one, relying on his personal judgment in matters of faith and customs which are linked to the establishment of Christian doctrine, shall dare to interpret the Sacred Scriptures either by twisting its text to his individual meaning in opposition to that which has been and is held by Holy Mother Church, whose function is to pass judgment on the true meaning and interpretation of the Sacred Scriptures; or by giving it meanings contrary to the unanimous consent of the fathers, even if interpretations of this kind were never intended for publication.

And in the next century an Eastern Orthodox confession expressed the correlation of Scripture and church in an effort at a balanced statement: "The Holy Scriptures were entrusted to the church by God, as a deposit of great treasure, so that we can think of the church as the guardian of and guide to the inspired Scriptures. . . . The Holy Scriptures are the truth, as they come from God, who is truth itself. And the church is their pillar and foundation [1 Tm 3.15], because it supports or guards the Scriptures and interprets them aright and defends them to the death."

As the "pillar," therefore, the church "has authority, in her general councils, to examine and warrant the Scripture."

According to Richard Arnold, there was a discernible "influence of Anglo-American Protestantism's anti-interpretive tradition on early constitutional hermeneutics," also because so many of the founders of the Republic and framers of the Constitution came out of the traditions of British Protestants and, among these Protestant groups, of Congregationalists and other English Dissenters. For, in the words of another constitutional scholar, H. Jefferson Powell, these Protestant "attacks on the legitimacy of scriptural interpretation spilled over easily into the political sphere." But it soon became clear, too, that neither in Protestantism nor in the early American Republic would it be possible to maintain the oxymoron of an "anti-interpretive tradition of interpretation," because the experience of textual interpretation in every community demonstrates that the only real alternative to hermeneutics is bad hermeneutics. Therefore it was in the second generation of the Reformation, with such massive works as the *Clavis Scripturae Sacrae* of 1567 by Matthias Flacius Illyricus, that a full-fledged exposition of hermeneutical method was called for.

In constitutional theory, too, the methodology of interpretation has repeatedly become a question and a *crux interpretum.* Oliver Wendell Holmes, Jr., in a brief essay published three years before he joined the Supreme Court, identified the central question when he defined: "Thereupon we ask, not what this man meant, but what those words would mean in the mouth of a normal speaker of English, using them in the circumstances in which they were used. . . . We do not inquire what the legislature *meant;* we ask only what the statute *means.*" As this was true of statutes, so it is true *a fortiori* of the United States Constitution, as one of the most thoughtful of its interpreters, Edward H. Levi, has proposed: "The influence of constitution worship. . . . gives great freedom to a court. It can always abandon what has been said in order to go back to the written document itself. It is a freedom greater than it would have had if no such document existed. . . . A written constitution must be enormously ambiguous in its general provisions. . . . A constitution cannot prevent change; indeed by permitting an appeal to the constitution, the discretion of the court is increased and change made possible." Interpretation—or rather "interpretations," in the plural—there will inevitably be, therefore. The question is: How to keep that "great freedom" of the court, as Levi terms it, from degenerating into a "freewheeling," as several scholars have termed it, and therefore capricious, and, in Charles Black's delightful epithet, "Humpty-Dumpty textual manipulation," a substitution of the *ipse dixit* of the court for the authority of what Justice Byron Raymond White called "textual support in the constitutional language" itself?

Richard H. Fallon has proposed a taxonomy of "five kinds of constitutional argument," for each of which it is not difficult to find similar arguments in the history of biblical interpretation:

1. arguments from the plain, necessary, or historical meaning of the constitutional text;
2. arguments about the intent of the framers;
3. arguments of constitutional theory that reason from the hypothesized purposes that best explain either particular constitutional provisions or the constitutional text as a whole;
4. arguments based on judicial precedent; and
5. value arguments that assert claims about justice or social policy.

Fallon then makes the case for his version of "a constructivist coherence theory of constitutional interpretation," in which these five forms of argument interact to form an interconnected whole.

When Richard A. Posner, professor of law and judge and Renaissance man, published the first edition of his fascinating book *Law and Literature* in 1988, as he reports ten years later in the second edition, "interpretation was a hot topic both in literary criticism . . . and in legal scholarship." In fact, as Richard A. Epstein put it in 1992, "The question of interpretation now enjoys the distinction of being the single most debated issue of constitutional law, surpassing the once dominant debate over the legitimacy of judicial review," even though, in Mark Tushnet's words, "for about thirty years, roughly from 1940 to 1970, interpretivism had a bad reputation." But by the time Posner wrote the second edition of his book in 1998, he was convinced that "the topic of interpretation has cooled in both fields." On balance, he continues, "the harvest of all that has been written about interpretation is meager. It comes down to two propositions": first, "interpretation is always relative to a purpose that is not given by the interpretive process itself but that is brought in from the outside and guides the process"; second, "interpretation is not much, and maybe not at all, improved by being made self-conscious, just as one doesn't become a better reader by studying linguistics." The second of these propositions will concern us in the chapter that follows. But does it not border on historical reductionism to speak in the first proposition of "a purpose that is not given by the interpretive process itself but that is brought in from the outside *and guides the process,*" as though this were "always" the decisive element, or even perhaps the only element, in the interpretation of a text?

Although a full consideration of the question goes beyond the scope of this book, there is also a need to "interpret the interpretations." "In interpreting a law," Justice David Davis declared in 1866, "the motives which must have operated with the legislature in passing it are proper to be considered." But Justice Holmes urged, as noted earlier, that "we do not inquire what the legislature *meant;* we ask only what the statute *means.*" Creeds and confessions have, in varying detail, set forth rules of scriptural hermeneutics, which are concerning us throughout this book. But the applications of the creeds and confessions to the life and teaching of the church has necessitated in addition the working out of rules of confessional hermeneutics.

"Outbreaks" and "Quiet Instants"

For when Henry James, in the novel that he himself regarded as "the best, 'all around' " of all his works, spoke about "the quiet instants that sometimes settle more matters than the outbreaks dear to the historic muse," he could have been criticizing how "the historic muse" has treated both the history of biblical interpretation and the history of constitutional interpretation. The first outbreak ever of theological debate over whether the body of Christ on the altar was identical with the body born of Mary, which took place in the Benedictine monastery at Corbie during the ninth century; the renewed outbreak of the controversy in the eleventh century, when the hapless Berengar of Tours, under duress, signed, then withdrew, and then signed again an affirmation of the doctrine of the real presence; the outbreak of the question of the presence as the most important dogmatic difference between the two main branches of the Protestant Reformation on the Continent, the Lutheran and the Reformed—these outbreaks are the stuff of which chapter titles and historical periodizations are made. But the quiet instants, virtually every day for nearly two thousand years and in more than two thousand languages, when communities all over the world have gathered around bread and wine and consecrated them with the biblical formula "This is my body" and "This is my blood," represent a continuity that "the historic muse" has all but ignored; for they are part of the description of the godly man that serves as a kind of epigraph for the Book of Psalms, and by extension for the whole of Scripture (and therefore for the first chapter of this book), "The law his meditation night and day" (Ps 1.2 NEB). These "quiet instants" of a "purpose that *is* given by the interpretive process itself," by liturgical celebration, and by meditation on the text, *pace* Posner's description, do have a part in guiding the process. The daily practice of the *lectio divina* was prescribed as a necessary component of the monastic life in the Middle Ages, but it is a central component of lay piety also in Protestantism, to the point of authenticating the canonical books of the Bible not by church authority but "by the testimony and inward illumination of the Holy Spirit, which enables us to distinguish them from other ecclesiastical books." The verse-by-verse exposition of the Sacred Text, in an exegetical course or in a series of homilies on the prescribed pericopes or in a commentary or in private meditation and study, begins with the text. Sometimes, moreover, it does so without any immediate consideration of the pertinence of this text to any specific "purpose that is not given by the interpretive process itself but that is brought in from the outside," but simply to carry out a religious or an academic assignment, often enough, if truth be told, in a rather perfunctory or ritualistic fashion. In the course of the assignment, such an outside "purpose" undeniably may come in to have its say, although it is certainly a great exaggeration to say that for every interpreter of every verse of every chapter it always "guides the process." "Apply yourself totally to the text, apply its total content to yourself [*Te totum applica ad textum: rem totam applica ad te*]": emblazoned as the epigraph for successive editions of the standard "Nestle" edition of the Greek New Testament, this motto of Johann Albrecht Bengel, whose "text and critical apparatus (1736) mark the beginning of modern scientific work in that field" and whose one-volume commentary, *Gnomon Novi Testamenti* of 1742, "remains a classic," is not only an idealized prescription of how the interpretation of Scripture ought to work in a perfect world (or in a perfect church), but an accurate description of how, at least sometimes, the chronological sequence does work in the experience of the individual biblical commentator or of the church.

But "commentary" as a method of verse-by-verse exposition, or as a genre or even as a title for a scholarly tome, is not confined to biblical exegesis, whether Jewish or Christian; in modern classical scholarship there are, for example, the commentary of Hornblower on Thucydides, the commentary of Gruber on Boethius, and countless others. Thomas Aquinas acquired the massive erudition he would need for composing the *Summa Theologica* through preparing commentaries on Aristotle marked by "a minute and closely literal analysis," and, as *magister in sacra pagina,* through composing similar commentaries on the books of the Bible, whose stated purpose it was "to treat the text, not by reference to the reader's own interests, difficulties, or enthusiasms, even if they are inspired by his faith, but rather according to the internal order governing the development of the text and the arrangement of its parts." Especially in the law, this method of study commends itself as a way of understanding any monumental text of jurisprudence. One of the classics of English legal thought is Sir William Blackstone's *Commentaries on the Law of England* of 1765–69, which was quoted in the pathbreaking case *Marbury* v. *Madison* of 1803 and in many Supreme Court cases since. The full subtitle of Daniel J. Boorstin's wise and instructive book of 1941 on the *Commentaries,* parodying the pleonastic style of book titles in Blackstone's time, is a similarly accurate description of the process of commentary in jurisprudence: "An essay on Blackstone's Commentaries showing how Blackstone, employing eighteenth-century ideas of science, religion, history, aesthetics, and philosophy, made of the law at once a conservative and a mysterious science." In individual decisions during his more than a third of a century on the Supreme Court, from 1811 to 1845, Justice Joseph Story did indeed frequently write a response to a case that had been "brought in from the outside," in which he often made his philosophical presuppositions quite clear, while at the same time voicing his "entire confidence, that it is consistent with the constitution and laws of the land." But he was also the author, in 1833, of *Commentaries on the Constitution of the United States,* reprinted several times since and quoted repeatedly over the decades in Supreme Court opinions, also articulating those philosophical presuppositions but proceeding article by article in a style of exegesis that is often reminiscent of biblical commentaries. A judge begins with a topical question or a complaint or an appeal, proceeding from that to the statutes and eventually, if necessary, all the way to the Constitution; and courses in torts or property law likewise start from collections of specific cases. But courses in constitutional law, whether in law school, college, or a program of continuing education, can also be designed as an *explication de texte,* in which the discussion of present-day questions of society and politics can and must be deferred until the words and phrases of the Constitution have been parsed just as carefully as they were composed, "anxiously and deliberately . . . clause by clause," as the Supreme Court said in 1859.

The same is true of the "quiet instants" in which a judge studies the Constitution before and after the "outbreaks" of dealing with particular cases, as well as between cases. Justice Hugo

Lafayette Black was known—and either admired or attacked—
for his strongly voiced opinions in several controversial cases,
among others *Korematsu* (1944) and *Griswold* (1965). But he was
also known for carrying a well-worn copy of the Constitution
around in his pocket, whipping it out at the slightest provocation,
and making "the law his meditation night and day." As he confessed (using this word *confess* in its creedal rather than in its
penitential sense), in a statement that he himself labeled "a confession of my articles of constitutional faith" and that, with only
the slightest of modifications, could have come from a champion
of biblical literalism: "That Constitution is my legal bible; its plan
of our government is my plan and its destiny my destiny. I cher-
ish every word of it, from the first to the last, and I personally
deplore even the slightest deviation from its least important com-
mands. I have thoroughly enjoyed my small part in trying to
preserve our Constitution with the earnest desire that it may meet
the fondest hope of its creators, which was to keep this nation
strong and great through countless ages."

The Ordinary and the Extraordinary Magisterium

To account for the puzzling, or even (to him, at any rate) trou-
bling, discovery "that there was no formal acknowledgment on
the part of the Church of the doctrine of the Holy Trinity till the
fourth [century]," namely, at the First Council of Nicaea in 325,
John Henry Newman formulated the axiom: "No doctrine is defined till it is violated." Without employing the technical terms,
he was speaking here about the authority that in nineteenth-
century Roman Catholic canon law and theology would come to
be called the *magisterium* of the church, a term with significant
precedent in conciliar and confessional usage. The magisterium
includes not only what Newman terms the "formal acknowledg-

ment" of a doctrine in the decree of an ecumenical council or in some other authoritative pronouncement, such as a creed or a confession of faith or a papal definition (often labeled the "extraordinary" magisterium of the church), but the ongoing communication of Christian doctrine as "what the church of Jesus Christ believes, teaches, and confesses on the basis of the word of God" every day in preaching, in worship, in catechesis, in theological instruction, and in print (the "ordinary" magisterium). In the language of the First Vatican Council, "by divine and Catholic faith all those things are to be believed which are contained in the word of God as found in Scripture and tradition, and which are proposed by the church as matters to be believed as divinely revealed, whether by her solemn [extraordinary] judgment or in her ordinary and universal magisterium." Newman's generalization meant that a doctrine that has already been believed all along by the faithful, taught in catechetical instruction, and confessed in the liturgy often achieves formal definition in a confession, creed, or conciliar decree only when it has been challenged, and therefore that councils, popes, bishops, and other agencies act to issue such a formal definition only when they finally must because they are faced with such a challenge. Newman could press this notion very far indeed, even to the point of asserting, concerning the Filioque doctrine that divided East and West precisely on the grounds of whether it conflicted with the tradition: "The doctrine of the Double Procession was no Catholic dogma in the first ages, though it was more or less clearly stated by individual Fathers; yet if it is now to be received, as surely it must be, as part of the Creed, it was really held everywhere from the beginning, and therefore, in a measure, held as a mere religious impression, and perhaps an unconscious one." The words quoted in the first chapter from another nineteenth-century source, "Neither patriarchs nor councils could have introduced novelties amongst us, because the protector of religion is the very body of the church, even the people themselves," aptly describe the distinction between the ordinary and the extraordinary magisterium. Included in the distinction is the recognition, as voiced by the Seventh Ecumenical Council, that "following the God-spoken teaching of our holy fathers and the tradition of the catholic church (for we recognize that this tradition comes from the Holy Spirit who dwells in her)" entails and includes both "written and unwritten tradition of the church." Under the impact of the modern historical-critical study of Bible and tradition, therefore, the extraordinary magisterium of the Roman Catholic Church in the early twentieth century felt obliged to condemn what it termed "the emancipation of exegesis from the [ordinary and extraordinary] magisterium of the church."

In its own version of that distinction, based on the cumulative interpretations of the "cases and controversies" clause of the Constitution (art. 3, sec. 2), the Supreme Court evolved, and then eventually systematized, a set of self-limiting guidelines for exercising the authority of its "extraordinary magisterium" to intervene in the "ordinary magisterium" or ongoing process of constitutional interpretation by other (and lower) jurisdictions. Chief Justice Roger Brooke Taney articulated the "duty" of such self-limitation in 1837:

> The court are fully sensible, that it is their duty, in exercising the high powers conferred on them by the constitution of the United States, to deal with these great and extensive interests, with the utmost caution; guarding, so far as they have the power to do so, the rights of property, and at the same time, carefully abstaining from any encroachment on the rights reserved to the states . . . [T]he court deem it proper to avoid volunteering an

opinion on any question, involving the construction of
the constitution, where the case itself does not bring the
question directly before them, and make it their duty to
decide upon it.

For that was the business of the "ordinary magisterium," represented by the lower courts and above all by the states, to whom
"the powers not delegated to the United States by the Constitution, nor prohibited by it to the States, are reserved" (amend.
10). Otherwise, according to Justice Samuel Freeman Miller in
the *Slaughterhouse Cases* of 1873, the Supreme Court would end
up becoming "a perpetual censor upon all legislation of the
States, on the civil rights of their own citizens." The Supreme
Court, Justice George Sutherland defined, "is without authority
to pass *abstract opinions* upon the constitutionality of acts of Congress." The emphasis here was on "abstract" opinions; for it remained true, as Justice Potter Stewart would put it in 1980, that
"in the exercise of its powers, Congress must obey the Constitution just as the legislatures of all the States must obey the Constitution in the exercise of their powers. If a law is unconstitutional, it is no less unconstitutional just because it is a product
of the Congress of the United States." Therefore "considerations
of propriety, as well as long-established practice," could be cited
as "demand[ing] that we refrain from passing upon the constitutionality of an act of Congress unless obliged to do so in the
proper performance of our judicial function, when the question
is raised by a party whose interests entitle him to raise it."

Quoting this latter formula, Justice Brandeis in 1936 applied
his keen powers of analysis and of synthesis to codifying "a series
of rules [that the Court has developed, for its own governance]
under which it has avoided passing upon a large part of all the

constitutional questions pressed upon it for decision." They were seven in number:

1. The Court will not pass upon the constitutionality of legislation in a friendly, non-adversary, proceeding, declining because to decide such questions "is legitimate only in the last resort, and as a necessity in the determination of real, earnest and vital controversy between individuals";

2. The Court will not "anticipate a question of constitutional law in advance of the necessity of deciding it";

3. The Court will not "formulate a rule of constitutional law broader than is required by the precise facts to which it is to be applied";

4. The Court will not pass upon a constitutional question although properly presented by the record, if there is also present some other ground upon which the case may be disposed of;

5. The Court will not pass upon the validity of a statute upon the complaint of one who fails to show that he is injured by its operation;

6. The Court will not pass upon the constitutionality of a statute at the instance of one who has availed himself of its benefits; and

7. "When the validity of an act of Congress is drawn in question, and even if a serious doubt of constitutionality is raised, it is a cardinal principle that this Court will first ascertain whether a construction of the statute is fairly possible by which the question may be avoided."

A few years later, a gloss by Justice Harlan Fiske Stone qualified Justice Brandeis's formulation of the ground rules by suggesting that "there may be narrower scope for operation of the presumption of constitutionality when legislation appears on its face to be within a specific prohibition of the Constitution, such as those of the first ten amendments, which are deemed equally specific when held to be embraced within the Fourteenth." On the basis of that importance it has been said that "the Fourteenth Amendment is a 'brooding omnipresence' over all state legislation."

Although it is true both of the Constitution and of the Bible that "no set of legal institutions or prescriptions exists apart from the narratives that locate it and give it meaning. For every constitution there is an epic, for each decalogue a scripture," one fundamental difference that would strike any reader even upon merely opening these two texts for the first time is that in the Bible the "narratives" and the "epic" predominate, and, in addition, that there are many different "literary genres," not merely the sorts of legal prescriptions and prohibitions that particularly the Pentateuch has in common with the Constitution. In spite of the similarities noted by Robert Burt, therefore, the parables of Jesus are radically different from constitutional injunctions in that they confront the interpreter with the literary challenge of discovering the point of comparison between the parable and its intended message; the parable of the sower is one of the very few in which that key is provided (Mt 13.18–23). The prophecies of Ezekiel, of Daniel, and of John in the Apocalypse summon up images of the cosmic war between good and evil and call men and nations to account before the judgment seat of God. Thereby they not only evoke from the defenders of apocalypticism in the modern era the hermeneutical insistence that "so far from being enshrouded in impenetrable mystery, it is that which especially constitutes the word of God a lamp to our feet and a light to our path," but make an article on the Last Judgment a necessary component also of many mainstream confessions and creeds, for which there was no equivalent in the Constitution. Much less, of course, does the Constitution have any counterpart to the erotic imagery of the Song of Songs, which had to be allegorized already within Judaism before the book could be admitted to the canon and which then went on in Christian exegesis to produce a rich allegorical literature, with Christ and the soul or Christ and the church being identified as the subjects of the exchanges between Bridegroom and Beloved.

Interpretive Ambiguities Shared by the Bible and the Constitution

Although the Bible is, therefore, a vastly more complicated and heterogeneous text than the American Constitution, they both present their interpreters with a confusing array of ambiguities when addressing any issue. As Justice Frankfurter once observed, in words that could apply equally to either text, "in dealing not with the machinery of government but with human rights, the absence of formal exactitude, or want of fixity of meaning, is not an unusual or even regrettable attribute of constitutional provisions. Words being symbols do not speak without a gloss." For "it is no very uncommon paradox in Western history," in an observation by Brian Tierney that applies to both these primal texts, "that the literal application by would-be reformers of half-understood old texts from a different historical epoch can have revolutionary implications for their own time."

Consequently there is from the outset the dilemma of deciding which of the several pertinent proof texts to apply to the specific issue at hand and of "explaining and reconciling apparently contradictory passages." At least theoretically, all of these proof texts in the Bible or in the Constitution possess equal authority, and they are believed to harmonize with one another. Therefore, as Justice Frankfurter said in a particularly delicate case, "The provisions of the Constitution which confer on the Congress and the President powers to enable this country to wage war are as much part of the Constitution as provisions looking to a nation at peace. . . . To talk about a military order that expresses an allowable judgment of war needs by those entrusted with the duty of conducting war as 'an unconstitutional order' is to suffuse a part of the Constitution [the duty of the President to wage war as 'commander in chief of the army and navy of the United States, and of the militia of the several states, when called into the actual service of the United States,' art. 2, sec. 2] with an atmosphere of unconstitutionality." Nevertheless, such provisions in both texts can also repeatedly be seen as overlapping or as conflicting—or even, in Justice Tom Clark's words, quoting an earlier decision, "as running 'almost into each other.' "

In the Gospel of John, for example, Jesus makes two contrasting statements about his relation to God the Father: "I and the Father are one [Greek *hen,* Vulg *unum*]" (Jn 10.30), that neuter singular being taken by such interpreters as Augustine to be proof of a single nature and the plural verb "are" as proof of a plurality of persons; but four chapters later, "the Father is greater than I" (Jn 14.28), from which "Arius and Eunomius . . . had taken this to imply a difference. From there they . . . introduced a difference in nature; but the difference of cause and effect [within the divine nature, *unum*] they denied once and for all, because they knew that it could not introduce any change of separation of nature anywhere, but would always keep the union of nature indivisible."

Again, one of the most extreme examples of this dilemma in the history of the creedal and confessional use of the Bible is at the center of the Reformation controversies over the doctrine of justification. As the premiere biblical example of faith and as "the father of all who believe" (Rom 4.11), Abraham "believed the Lord, and He reckoned it to him as righteousness" (Gn 15.6). In his Epistle to the Romans the apostle Paul cites this example and quotes these words from Genesis for his exposition of the doctrine of justification (Rom 4.3), proving that "a man is justified by faith apart from works of law"—or even, in Luther's translation, "ohne des Gesetzes Werke, *allein* durch den Glauben," by faith alone (Rom 3.28). But the Epistle of James quotes the same words from Genesis to prove "that faith was active along with his works, and faith was completed by works," so that "a man is justified by works and not by faith alone" (Jas 2.22–24). A concentration on the proof texts from Romans underlies the Protestant doctrine of justification by faith, and even justification by faith alone (*sola fide*), but the authority of Scripture makes it necessary to reconcile or harmonize the two texts: "James does not contradict anything in this doctrine of ours," a Protestant confession insists; "for he speaks of an empty, dead faith. . . . James said that works justify, yet without contradicting the apostle [Paul]." Rejecting this interpretation, the Council of Trent blended references to Paul, to James, and to other biblical books in formulating its doctrine of justification; and it anathematized the Protestant doctrine "that by that faith alone are forgiveness and justification effected." And in an Eastern Orthodox confession responding to the Protestant Reformation, the first two proof texts came from James.

Sometimes, as in the case of the two passages from the Gospel of John, the proof texts can be located very close together, but the choice between them is, if anything, all the more difficult for that reason. An important constitutional illustration of this dilemma appears within the text of the First Amendment. Its formulations of the "freedom of press, freedom of speech, freedom of religion"—listing them in that order, in a reversal of the Constitution's order of religion, speech, and press—were once described by Justice William O. Douglas as holding a "preferred position" among all the constitutional freedoms: "Congress shall make no law respecting an establishment of religion, or prohibiting the free exercise thereof; or abridging the freedom of spech, or of the press." Yet when the speech or press whose freedom was alleged to have been abridged was concerned with expressing religious faith, in this case the right of Jehovah's Witnesses to distribute their tracts, the Supreme Court in 1938 elected to treat the case under free speech rather than under freedom of religion, even though the First Amendment singles out religion from among all other possible forms of expression and accords it separate treatment, mentioning it in its first clause. Even within that first clause, moreover, the injunction against any "law respecting an establishment of religion"—which, in Leonard Levy's apt phrase, "functions to protect religion from government, and government from religion"—is potentially in tension with the injunction against any "law . . . prohibiting the free exercise thereof." In the sharp formulation of Justice Potter Stewart, "while in many contexts the Establishment Clause and the Free Exercise Clause fully complement each other, there are areas in which a doctrinaire reading of the Establishment Clause leads to irreconcilable conflict with the Free Exercise Clause." Recognizing that "these two clauses may in certain instances overlap" or even seemingly "conflict," the Court has repeatedly had to interpret one of them in such a way as not to run afoul of the other.

Ratified less than two years apart, the Fourteenth Amendment (July 1868) and the Fifteenth Amendment (February 1870) were both intended to forbid any state to "abridge the privileges or immunities of citizens of the United States" (amend. 14, sec.

1), specifically "the right of citizens of the United States to vote" (amend. 15, sec. 1). But the unanimous decision of the Supreme Court in 1927, striking down the exclusion of blacks from voting in a state Democratic primary, based itself on the Fourteenth Amendment and "[found] it unnecessary to consider the Fifteenth Amendment," even though it was the Fifteenth Amendment, on "the right of citizens of the United States to vote," over which the litigating sides had originally been disputing. A later decision on the same issue in 1944 did invoke "the well-established principle of the Fifteenth Amendment" to declare any all-white primary unconstitutional. But after Justice Frankfurter, for the Court, ruled that "when a legislature thus singles out a readily isolated segment of a racial minority for special discriminatory treatment, it violates the Fifteenth Amendment," Justice Charles Evans Whittaker, concurring in the conclusion of the Court but filing a separate opinion, urged "that the decision should be rested not on the Fifteenth Amendment, but rather on the Equal Protection Clause of the Fourteenth Amendment to the Constitution." In another case also involving a choice between the Fourteenth Amendment and another amendment, in this case the First, Justice Owen Roberts, for the Court, ultimately based his opinion on the First Amendment, but Justice Harlan Fiske Stone relied on the Fourteenth instead.

These examples illustrate another underlying interpretive ambiguity in both texts, namely, that both of them lack any explicit prescription for the correct method of interpretation. That lack becomes especially visible through an examination of the history of the interpretation of the Bible by hindsight, from the perspective of the history of Christian exegesis. In combination with another passage from the Pauline epistles, "The letter kills, but the spirit gives life" (2 Cor 3.6), the statement "Now this is an allegory" (Gal 4.24), introducing the allegory of Sarah and Hagar, has proved to be one of the most productive in the subsequent interpretation of the Bible. As many of the great exegetical masters have documented, the Bible allows for or requires, and sometimes itself practices, allegorical exegesis, not merely extrapolation: how else could such imprecatory passages as Psalm 137.9, "Happy shall be he who takes your little ones and dashes them against the rock!" have been retained in the church's liturgy? The Constitution does not do so, although critics of one or another Supreme Court decision have sometimes accused it of allegorization. Yet, with few if any exceptions, exegetes have nevertheless made the *sensus literalis* primary, so that the life of Christ is not to be allegorized out of history. After a lengthy catalog of *gravamina* against the pope and the Council of Trent that in some ways sounds like the list of grievances against King George III in the American Declaration of Independence, the Calvinistic *King's Confession,* which was issued in Scotland in 1581, concluded: "And finally, we detest all his vain *allegories,* rites, signs and traditions brought into the church without or against the word of God." But that generalized antipathy to allegory in favor of the *sensus literalis* did not prevent another, nearly contemporary Reformed confession, in its doctrine of the eucharistic presence, from "reject[ing] those ridiculous interpreters who insist on what they call the precise literal sense of the solemn words of the supper—'This is my body, this is my blood.' For without question we hold that they are to be taken figuratively, so that the bread and wine are said to *be* that which they *signify.*"

Absolute or "Contemporary Community Standards"?

Yet another interpretive dilemma shared by the Constitution and the Bible is that they are both involved in "a clash of absolutes," a tension between their enunciation of absolute and universally binding principles and their use of an almost statistical criterion like "unusual" (amend. 8), or their acknowledgment of the force of "contemporary community standards." That phrase acquired normative status in 1957 when the Court formulated the definition of "obscenity" on this basis: "whether to the average person, applying contemporary community standards, the dominant theme of the material taken as a whole appeals to prurient interest." But fifteen years later, as the next stage in "the somewhat tortured history of the Court's obscenity decisions" — as the opinion of the Supreme Court itself acknowledged it to be — the Court held that "it is neither realistic nor constitutionally sound to read the First Amendment as requiring that the people of Maine or Mississippi accept public depiction of conduct found tolerable in Las Vegas, or New York City." In his dissent Justice William O. Douglas rejected these "vague tests" as "the standards we ourselves have written into the Constitution." On this basis, obscenity was said to be defined by *local* not national standards, not to say by some sort of "eternal verities." But what happens to the interpretation when "contemporary community standards" have changed?

To stay with the standards of sexual mores and with what have come to be referred to as "gender issues": when the apostle Paul charges the church at Corinth with harboring "immorality [*porneia*] . . . of a kind that is not found even among pagans, for a man is living with his father's wife" (1 Cor 5.1), a relationship that was forbidden not only by the Mosaic law (Lv 18.8) as incest, but by the pagan Roman law, and, according to *The Cambridge Platform,* was also "condemned by the light of nature," he seems to be introducing the criterion of "contemporary community standards" or of "natural law" or both. And a catechism-confession of the sixteenth century justified compulsory instruction in the Ten Commandments (including "Thou shalt not commit adultery") for all citizens regardless of church affiliation on the basis that the civil government has a legitimate right to "insist that the people learn to know how to distinguish between right and wrong *according to the standards of those among whom they live and make their living.*" But what happens when, at some later time or in another culture as investigated by voyages of discovery or by anthropology, such "immorality . . . *is* found among pagans" or no longer even counts as immorality, because the "standards of those among whom they live" have shifted? Again, is Paul's prescription that a woman must veil her head at worship but that a man must not cover his head, on the basis of a standard that was regarded as *prepon* ("proper" or "fitting") then and there in the community of Corinth (1 Cor 11.2–16), to be taken as a standard that is permanently binding on all Christian worship communities everywhere? And what of the prohibition (1 Tm 2.12), "I permit no woman to teach or to have authority over men; she is to keep silent"? As it stands, this is based on the order of creation — "Adam was formed first, then Eve" (1 Tm 2.13) — and not on "contemporary community standards"; and it is invoked, in some Protestant confessions, in opposition to the Roman Catholic practice permitting baptism by a woman in a case of emergency. The recognition, in *The Irish Articles* of 1615, not only that "the law given from God by Moses as touching ceremonies and rites be abolished, and the civil precepts thereof be not of necessity to be received in any commonwealth," but that "there be some hard things in the Scriptures . . . as have proper relation to the times in which they were first uttered," seems to imply that by some criterion or other it is possible to identify these "hard things" that do not "have proper relation" to later times, but only "to the times in which they were first uttered." The same question arises with the language of *The Second Helvetic Confession,* quoted earlier, about considering "the circum-

stances in which [statements in Scripture] were set down." Answering such questions as these and interpreting the pertinent
proof texts goes even beyond the prescription (which has itself
proved to be easier to formulate than it is to apply) that in reading the Bible "a Christian . . . acteth differently upon that which
each particular passage thereof containeth."

These appeals of the New Testament to the authority, apart
from the word of revelation, of what is "proper" (1 Cor 11.13)
and of what is "done decently and in order" (1 Cor 14.40), or of
the Supreme Court, apart from the word of the Constitution, to
"contemporary community standards" or even to "the general
principles of law and reason," raise in both areas the mooted
range of questions associated with the concept of natural law. Is
there an "eternal, objective, and universal law," and is it knowable
without special revelation (as the eighteenth-century critics of the
church insisted more vigorously than the church did)? It was the
Declaration of Independence, not the Constitution, that justified
its arguments on the basis of "the laws of Nature, and of Nature's
God"; and the absence from the text of the Constitution of any
explicit parallel to this justification, or of any other even vaguely
theistic point of reference, has often served as the basis for arguments from silence on various sides of those questions. These
reasonings have proved to be as inconclusive as such arguments
ex silentio usually are, but they have not excluded natural law and
natural right from the vocabulary of arguments in the Court.
When, in the nineteenth century, the Supreme Court was told
that "the legislative power is restrained and limited by the principles of natural justice," this appeal to natural law was able to
base itself on the authority of an eighteenth-century decision of
the Court that had in turn been based on "the general principles
of law and reason."

The classic formulation of those "general principles of law

and reason" in Christian Scripture was the statement of Paul in the Epistle to the Romans: "When Gentiles who have not the law do by nature what the law requires, they are a law to themselves, even though they do not have the law. They show that what the law requires is written on their hearts" (Rom 2.14–15). On that basis the interpretation of the revealed law of God and the practice of church discipline could include what *The Cambridge Platform* identified as offenses "condemned by the light of nature." It was ostensibly on this basis that blasphemy came to be a civil offense, not only a sin, although, as Leonard Levy has shown, this principle, once established, could be stretched to include a great variety of other offenses. From the Roman Catholic assertion that the church has the charge not only "to announce and authentically teach that truth which is in Christ," but also "and at the same time to give authoritative statement and confirmation of the principles of the moral order which derive from human nature itself" apart from specific revelation, it was another long step (or several) to the teachings of the Protestant Social Gospel urging "the recognition of the Golden Rule and the mind of Christ as the supreme law of society and the sure remedy of all social ills," and to the insistence not only on *natural* justice but on the "positive witness that the *Christian* principles of justice and love should have full expression in all relationships whatsoever—personal, industrial, business, civic, national, and international."

The Final Arbiter

The Bible and the Constitution likewise have in common—although it often comes as a surprise to laity in both law and theology that this is so—an ambiguity regarding which specific entity possesses the authority to provide the definitive interpretation of the normative Scripture. Reading the New Testament *a posteriori* in the light of church history for its directives or precedents about the authoritative interpreter of its own text, or of the sacred text as a whole, we find at least the following possibilities:

1. The first instance of (using the language of the Constitution, art. 3, sec. 2) "cases" and "controversies" to arise in the early church after Pentecost was the case of the Levitical laws and the controversy over their applicability to Gentile converts. To deal with the controversy, an appeal was made to the authority of "the apostles and elders gathered together [in Jerusalem] to consider this question" (Acts 15.6). Peter, Paul, and Barnabas appeared before the assembly in support of the case against obliging Gentiles to be circumcised and to observe the kosher dietary laws. "After they finished speaking, James replied, 'Brethren, listen to me' " (Acts 15.13), and the gathering formulated a letter opening with the formula "It has seemed good to the Holy Spirit and to us" (Acts 15.28), which is identified in the following chapter as "the *dogmata* which had been reached by the apostles and elders who were at Jerusalem" (Acts 16.4). "After whose example" of identifying their legislation with the will of the Holy Spirit, as one confession put it, "other orthodox councils have, in the same style, concluded their decrees." As the Second Council of Constantinople phrased it in 553, quoting that formula from Acts 15, "Even though the grace of the Holy Spirit was abundant in each of the apostles, so that none of them required the advice of another in order to do his work, nevertheless they were loathe to come to a decision on the issue of the circumcision of Gentiles until they had met together to test their various opinions against the witness of the Holy Scriptures." In the context of a divided Christendom, this could even be taken by the East to mean that

"an ecumenical council is not only above the pope but above any council of his," a position that the Western defenders of papal authority of course vigorously opposed.

2. At the same time, however, it was clear from the New Testament that although the spokesman for this first "church council" at Jerusalem was James, "the Lord's brother" (Gal 1.19), Peter was in fact the only one of the twelve disciples whom Christ himself had singled out for special standing, in words that are emblazoned around the ceiling of the Roman basilica that bears his name: "Thou [singular] art Peter [*Petros*], and upon this rock [*petra*] I will build my church; and the gates of hell shall not prevail against it" (Mt 16.18 AV). That passage was interpreted by the First Vatican Council to mean "that, according to the Gospel evidence, a primacy of jurisdiction over the whole church of God was immediately and directly promised to the blessed apostle Peter and conferred on him by Christ the Lord." From this it followed that "whoever succeeds to the chair of Peter obtains, by the institution of Christ himself, the primacy of Peter over the whole church." And therefore "we teach and declare that, by divine ordinance, the Roman church possesses a preeminence of ordinary power over every other church." To its rehearsal of these historic prerogatives the First Vatican Council of 1870 then added, "as a divinely revealed dogma, that when the Roman pontiff speaks *ex cathedra,* that is, when, in the exercise of his office as shepherd and teacher of all Christians, in virtue of his supreme apostolic authority, he defines a doctrine concerning faith and morals to be held by the whole church, he possesses, by the divine assistance promised to him in blessed Peter, that infallibility which the divine Redeemer willed his church to enjoy in defining doctrine concerning faith or morals."

3. But Christ had also made other promises about protecting his church against error, most notably: "The Counselor [*parak-*

lētos], the Holy Spirit, whom the Father will send in my name, he will teach you all things, and bring to your remembrance all that I have said to you" (Jn 14.26). Who is meant by this "you" — the apostles, most especially in their function as the inspired writers of the New Testament? their legitimate successors, whether in an ecumenical council or in the papacy, as just noted? or individual believers, by virtue of their faith, usually "in a due use of the ordinary means," but sometimes even "directly, without means"?

The language of the modern Supreme Court may sometimes inadvertently give the impression that in its constitutional charter there is no similar ambiguity. In 1958, for example, Chief Justice Earl Warren, speaking for the Court, said that it was "respected by this Court and the Country as a permanent and indispensable feature of our constitutional system" that "the federal judiciary is supreme in the exposition of the law of the Constitution"; and in 1962, speaking for the Court, Justice William Brennan declared that "deciding whether a matter has in any measure been committed by the Constitution to another branch of government, or whether the action of that branch exceeds whatever authority has been committed, is itself a delicate exercise in constitutional interpretation, and is a responsibility of this Court as ultimate interpreter of the Constitution." In this consensus they were expressing what has become the standard view of the authority of the Supreme Court in relation to the Constitution. But "it is a singular fact that the State constitutions did not give this power to the judges in express terms," and that the United States Constitution itself did not spell out that authority either. It did prescribe that "the judicial power of the United States, shall be vested in one supreme court, and in such inferior courts as the Congress may from time to time ordain and establish" (art. 3, sec. 1), and it did stipulate the several types of cases to which this "judicial power shall extend," including "all cases, in law and eq-

uity, arising under this constitution" (art. 3, sec. 2). But that did
not quite include, in so many words, the authority that Justice
Brennan described as the "responsibility of this Court as ultimate
interpreter of this Constitution." In fixing that responsibility, the
"notable case," as Chief Justice Warren called it, was *Marbury* v.
Madison in 1803. According to the concluding paragraph of the
unanimous opinion of the Court in *Marbury,* delivered by Chief
Justice Marshall, *"the particular phraseology* of the constitution of
the United States confirms and strengthens the principle, supposed to be essential to *all written constitutions,* that a law repugnant to the constitution is void; and that courts, as well as other
departments, are bound by that instrument." Thus, by "logical
sequence," the argument was based simultaneously on the nature
of "all written constitutions" in general and on "the particular
phraseology" of article 3 of the American Constitution. Alexander
Hamilton had already anticipated in considerable detail the content of *Marbury* in *Federalist* 78. But the continuing scholarly
controversy about "judicial review" and its limits, especially during the twentieth century, has disclosed how much ambiguity
there still is, even after *Marbury.*

Yet the fact remains that in spite of any such seemingly un-
qualified assertions expressed in the concepts of "judicial review"
or of "papal infallibility," those who thus bear the supreme authority for interpreting the Great Code, whether of the Constitution or of the Bible, are, as "judicial officers," themselves
"bound by oath or affirmation, to support this constitution" (art.
6), and they repeat the oath prescribed by the Constitution for
the President, to "preserve, protect and defend the constitution
of the United States" (art. 2, sec. 1). Similarly, in the words of
the Second Vatican Council, "when the Roman pontiff or the
body of bishops together with him define a decision [which they
are said to do infallibly], they do so in accordance with the rev-

elation itself, *by which all are obliged to abide and to which all must conform.*"

Many of the differences and analogies between the Bible and the Constitution that have been discussed in the two chapters that constitute the first half of this book also raise, in one way or another, the fundamental problem of the relation between the authority of the original text and the authority of developing doctrine in the ongoing life and history of the community, to which the two chapters of the second half will be devoted.

The *Sensus Literalis* and the Quest for Original Intent

Scripture cannot be set aside (Jn 10.35 NEB)

The Spirit and the Letter

The statement quoted earlier from Justice Holmes, about the interpretive problems involved in employing the Constitution to answer questions that "could not have been foreseen completely by the most gifted of its begetters," finds a rather unexpected corroboration and parallel in a description by the New Testament of how, after they had written down their prophecies under divine inspiration, the Old Testament "prophets . . . inquired what person or time was indicated by the Spirit of Christ within them" (1 Pt 1.10–11), probing their own writings to find some deeper meaning, which they could not have completely foreseen on their own when they originally set them down. For both texts, therefore, there must be a "spirit" that is present within—and yet that somehow lies beyond—the "letter" (2 Cor 3.6). Not "a knowledge according to the letter" but a knowledge according to the spirit was required. Quoting the words of Paul, "The letter kills, but the spirit gives life" (2 Cor 3.6), one sixteenth-century Reformed confession devoted a special paragraph to this distinction under the heading "Of the Spirit and the Letter"; but its primary emphasis was not on its implication for the interpretation of Scripture but on the contrast between "the spirit" as "the preaching of the gospel" and "the letter," which "signifies . . . especially the doctrine of the law." The Council of Trent, too, made a point of emphasizing the inadequacy of "the letter of the law." When it came to the interpretation of Scripture, it was Reformed doctrine that "the infallible rule of interpretation of Scripture is the Scripture itself; and therefore, when there is a question about the true and full sense of any Scripture (which is not manifold, but one), it must be searched and known by other places that speak more clearly." That interpretation—"not manifold, but one"—was the *sensus literalis* and the original intent of the passage.

But *sensus literalis* does not simply mean the same as "the literal sense," certainly not the same as "the literalistic sense," over which there has been so much controversy, particularly in the interpretation of the first chapters of the Book of Genesis in relation to Galileo or to Darwin. When Augustine undertook his *De Genesi ad litteram,* one of the several commentaries he wrote on the first book of the Bible in whole or in part, his exposition *ad litteram* did not prevent him from seeking the "spiritual sense"—and interpreting the "days" of the creation narrative as a single instant rather than as days in the literal sense of what we would call twenty-four hours. Therefore, by a *reductio ad absurdum:* When the fourth petition of the Lord's Prayer asks, "Give us this day our daily bread" (Mt 6.11), is the original intent and *sensus literalis* of the petition to be taken to be only "bread" rather than "everything required to satisfy our bodily needs, such as food and clothing, house and home, fields and flocks, money and property; a pious spouse and good children, trustworthy servants, godly and faithful rulers, good government, seasonable weather, peace and health, order and honor, true friends, faithful neighbors, and the like," which a later confession by a vigorous advocate of the *sensus literalis* takes to be the answer to the question "What does this *mean?*" to pray for daily bread, not merely "What does the term 'daily bread' *suggest* to you by free association or according to the spiritual sense?"

Because, in words quoted by Justice John Marshall Harlan, "the letter of the law is the body; the sense and reason of the law is the soul," that "spirit" or "soul," moreover, had to be discernible to later readers of the "letter," or at any rate to some of them. On the basis of the words of the Constitution, "The Congress shall have power . . . To make all laws which shall be necessary and proper for carrying into execution the foregoing powers, and all other powers vested by this constitution in the government of the United States, or in any department or officer thereof" (art. 1, sec. 8), Chief Justice Marshall issued the familiar prescription: "Let the end be legitimate, let it be within the scope of the constitution, and all means which are appropriate, which are plainly adapted to that end, which are not prohibited, but consist with *the letter and spirit* of the constitution, are constitutional." Or, in an early statement of the Christian rule of faith by Origen of Alexandria,

> Then there is the doctrine that the Scriptures . . . have not only that meaning which is obvious, but also another which is hidden from the majority of readers. For the contents of Scripture are the outward forms of certain mysteries and the images of divine things. On this point the entire church is unanimous, that while the whole law is spiritual, the inspired meaning is not rec-

ognized by all, but only by those who are gifted with the grace of the Holy Spirit in the word of wisdom and knowledge.

Commenting on Origen's typology, Jean Daniélou explains that although "the Old Testament . . . represents a system which is done away with, yet the Church . . . does not reject it; she preserves it, simply because it contains the type of Christ. But the carnal man, the slave of the letter, is incapable by himself of deciphering this. . . . Christ himself must grant that spiritual understanding." That is the hermeneutic underlying John Henry Newman's axiom: "It may be almost laid down as an historical fact, that the mystical interpretation and orthodoxy will stand or fall together." But what are the limits of this spiritual and "mystical" sense, and is it governed by any rules?

The *Sensus Plenior:* Radiations, Penumbras, Allegories, "Analogical Extensions"

In the interpretation of American Scripture or of Christian Scripture, it has always been necessary to go beyond the *sensus literalis* to find the *sensus plenior,* the "fuller meaning," also because, as Paul Brest has said, "strict textualism and intentionalism are not synergistic, but rather mutually antagonistic approaches to interpretation." That is true even of a definition of authority that encompasses what "is either expressly set down in Scripture, *or by good and necessary consequence may be deduced from Scripture.*" Whether in the interpretation of Christian Scripture or of American Scripture, such "deducing by good and necessary consequence" calls for "analogical extensions," by which a particular provision is extended to situations that are not identical but clearly analogous. "Congress shall make no law . . . abridging the

freedom . . . of the press" (amend. 1) was written to protect print-
ing presses as they were being operated by printers like Benjamin
Franklin at the end of the eighteenth century. But each successive
technology of communication, from presses driven by electrical
power to radio broadcasting to television to the Internet and
electronic publishing, has evoked a somewhat different analogical
extension of freedom of the press or of speech; and because
"speech will not be free if these are not also free," there is no end
in sight. Already in 1870, Justice William Strong had used the
language of "deduction" and "inference" to argue that "it is
not indispensable to the existence of any power claimed for the
Federal government that it can be found specified in the words
of the Constitution, or clearly and directly traceable to some
one of its specified powers. Its existence may be *deduced* fairly
from more than one of the substantive powers expressly defined,
or from them all combined. It is allowable to group together
any number of them and *infer* from them all that the power
claimed has been conferred." But in 1919, Justice Oliver Wendell
Holmes, Jr., although insisting, as he often did, that a case
"must be considered in the light of our whole experience and
not merely in that of what was said a hundred years ago" in the
literal text of the Constitution and its amendments, ridiculed the
idea of basing such a consideration on "some invisible radiation
from the general terms of the Tenth Amendment." In 1952, Justice Hugo L. Black voiced a similar polemic against vagueness
when he attacked an argument of Justice Felix Frankfurter for
invoking a "nebulous standard." Constitutional interpretation
could not be based on a foundation that was "invisible" or "nebulous."

Nevertheless, in a metaphor that was, if not "nebulous," then
only slightly different from the "invisible radiation" derided by
Holmes (and that must remind a patristic scholar of the meta-

physical language of Valentinian Gnosticism or Plotinian Neo-platonism), Justice Douglas, writing for the majority in *Griswold* to defend the drawing out of constitutional implications such as, above all, "the right of privacy" from the Bill of Rights, declared: "Specific guarantees in the Bill of Rights have penumbras, formed by emanations from those guarantees that help give them life and substance," so that "various guarantees create zones of privacy." For example, he argued, "the First Amendment has a penumbra where privacy is protected from governmental intrusion . . . , and while it is not expressly included in the First Amendment its existence is necessary in making the express guarantees fully meaningful." That made it constitutional. The metaphor caught on: "I agree fully with the Court that . . . the right of privacy is a fundamental personal right, *emanating* 'from the totality of the constitutional scheme under which we live,' " Justice Goldberg added in his opinion in *Griswold,* although in the same opinion he could argue that "these statements of Madison and Story make clear that *the Framers did not intend* that the first eight amend-ments be construed to exhaust the basic and fundamental rights which the Constitution guaranteed to the people." But dissenting from the majority in *Griswold,* Justice Hugo L. Black, with his customary adherence to the *ipsissima verba* and therefore the *sensus literalis* of the Constitution, found himself "unable to stretch the Amendment": "I get nowhere in this case," he explained, explic-itly citing Justice Douglas's metaphor, "by talk about a constitu-tional 'right of privacy' as an *emanation* from one or more con-stitutional provisions."

An especially creative illustration of how such a "penumbra" could be seen as "emanating" from a biblical text occurs in the bull *Unam Sanctam,* issued by Pope Boniface VIII in 1302. The biblical text was the brief exchange between Jesus and his disci-ples in the Garden of Gethsemane (Lk 22.38): "And they said,

'Look, Lord, here are two swords.' And he said to them, 'It is enough.' " But the term "sword" is also the metaphor for political authority in the standard New Testament proof text on that subject, "He does not bear the sword in vain" (Rom 13.4). Combining these sayings of Jesus and the disciples about "two swords" as "enough" with that New Testament metaphor, *Unam Sanctam* could employ them as the biblical warrant for the following argument:

> We learn from the words of the Gospel that in this church and in her power are two swords, the spiritual and the temporal. For when the apostles said, "Behold, here" (that is, in the church, since it was the apostles who spoke) "are two swords"—the Lord did not reply, "It is too much," but "It is enough." Truly he who denies that the temporal sword is in the power of Peter, misunderstands the words of the Lord (Jn 18.11), "Put up thy sword into the sheath."
>
> Both are in the power of the church, the spiritual sword and the material. But the latter is to be used *for* the church, the former *by* her; the former by the priest, the latter by kings and captains but at the will and by the permission of the priest. The one sword, then, should be under the other, and temporal authority subject to spiritual. . . .
>
> If, therefore, the earthly power can err, it shall be judged by the spiritual. . . . But if the supreme power err, it can only be judged by God, not by man. . . .
>
> Furthermore, we declare, state, define, and pronounce that it is altogether necessary to salvation for every human creature to be subject to the Roman pontiff.

This interpretation of "two swords" summarized the doctrine of papal power and, in the language of Pope Gregory VII, its "right to depose emperors," as this doctrine had developed in the conflicts of the eleventh, twelfth, and thirteenth centuries. But in *Unam Sanctam* the traditional doctrine attained its classic exegetical formulation.

In opposition, a Reformation confession denounced as "false, impious, tyrannical, and injurious to the church" this article of faith that the pope "by divine right possesses both swords, that is, the authority to bestow and transfer kingdoms." Another confession charged that this "improperly confused the power of the church with the power of the sword," even as it nevertheless affirmed, on the basis of the words of the New Testament, "He does not bear the sword in vain" (Rom 13.4), the doctrine of just war and the right of Christians to keep and bear arms and to hold political office. A Mennonite confession, which denied this, likewise used the biblical metaphor of "the sword," but quoted the words of the Gospel cited in *Unam Sanctam,* "Put your sword into its sheath" (Jn 18.11), against all use of force and violence by the church or the individual Christian. At the opposite extreme, one Reformed confession declared that God "has put the sword into the hands of magistrates to suppress crimes against the first as well as against the second table of the [Ten] Commandments," making blasphemy and false doctrine a civil offense. And with a clear allusion to—and a revision of—the tradition represented by *Unam Sanctam,* the Second Vatican Council in *Dignitatis humanae* cited the same narrative from the Gospels (Mt 26.51–53; Jn 18.36) to declare that Christ's "kingdom is not upheld by the sword," even as it acknowledged that "at times in the life of the people of God, as it has pursued its pilgrimage through the twists and turns of human history, there have been ways of acting hardly in tune with the spirit of the gospel, indeed contrary to it."

Such a broadening of biblical authority, for example by the Second Council of Nicaea and by the Council of Trent, by appeal to alleged "unwritten traditions," and of constitutional authority to include the quest for alleged "penumbras, formed by emanations from those guarantees that help give them life and substance," which, "while . . . not expressly included," are "necessary in making the express guarantees fully meaningful," have repeatedly called forth within both interpretive communities an appeal to the higher judgment of primitive authority, original intent, and the *sensus literalis*. Thus the conclusion of one of the three Reformation confessions presented to the Diet of the Holy Roman Empire in 1530 expressed the hope that "Christ's doctrine, the parent of all righteousness and salvation, may be properly considered, may be purged of all errors, and may be offered *in its native form* to all who love godliness and the true worship of God," for that "native form" was believed to be the purest. In the opening words of *The Irish Articles of Religion* of 1615, "the ground of our religion and the rule of faith and all saving truth is the word of God, contained in the Holy Scripture" as the original deposit of divine revelation, not any tradition, be it ever so authoritative or ancient. For American Scripture likewise, the power to decide was said to lie in the superior authority of the original, an authority that Justice Byron Raymond White labeled "textual support in the constitutional language." This authority may be seen as combining the first and the second in Richard H. Fallon's framework of interpretive theories, as enumerated earlier: "arguments from the plain, necessary, or historical meaning of the constitutional text" and "arguments about the intent of the framers."

"Eyewitnesses from the Beginning": The Originalist Impulse

Both the New Testament and the Constitution are set within historical periods that are endowed with a special aura by their traditions and that carry a unique authority for their communities. For the New Testament, it is the authority not alone of sacred "words not taught by human wisdom but taught by the Spirit" and therefore divinely inspired (1 Cor 2.13), but of sacred events, above all the life and teaching, crucifixion and resurrection, of Jesus Christ. "Those who from the beginning were eyewitnesses" (Lk 1.2) to those sacred events possessed a special standing already in the first and second Christian generations: "That which was from the beginning, which *we* have heard, which *we* have seen with our eyes, which *we* have looked upon and touched with our hands . . . that which *we* have seen and heard *we* proclaim also to you," the First Catholic Epistle of John opened (1 Jn 1.1–3). That special standing was acknowledged also by those New Testament writers who could not themselves lay claim to this title of "eyewitnesses from the beginning" and who therefore were obliged to privilege those who could. The apostle Paul, who was not an "eyewitness" in that sense, nevertheless laid great emphasis on his having "seen Jesus our Lord" (1 Cor 9.1) in a special personal appearance on the Damascus road (Acts 22.6–10; 26.13–18), even though he had not "known Christ after the flesh" (2 Cor 5.16 AV). Therefore he insisted, in response to his detractors and in the salutations of most of his epistles, that he was an authentic "apostle—not from men nor through man, but through Jesus Christ and God the Father" (Gal 1.1), who had been sent by Christ to the church, which was "built upon the foundation of the apostles and prophets, Jesus Christ himself being the chief cornerstone" (Eph 2.20). Amid all the claims in subsequent centuries of an "apostolic" primacy for the papal see of Rome or for the patriarchal see of Constantinople, therefore, the see of Jerusalem—not declared "patriarchal" until the Council of Chalcedon in 451—could still be acclaimed, even in an Eastern Orthodox confession that assigned to tradition an authority alongside that of Scripture, as "without doubt the mother and princess of all other churches," the church that "outshone all other churches in sanctity of doctrine and manners," because it was closest to the origins of the entire church in Christ and the disciples, regardless of what its condition may have become by the seventeenth century. Another Eastern Orthodox confession, moreover, could open with the declaration that "the holy, evangelical, and divine gospel of salvation should be set forth by all *in its original simplicity*" and with an appeal to the authority of those who were "ear- and eye-witnesses," even though it closed with an appeal to "the succession of our holy divine fathers and predecessors beginning from the apostles, and those whom the apostles appointed their successors, to this day, forming one unbroken chain."

But when, in the confessions of the Protestant Reformation, that authority of tradition was rejected in the name of *sola Scriptura,* this unique standing of the original and authentic Scripture in its *sensus literalis* rose accordingly: "The supreme judge by which all controversies of religion are to be determined, and all decrees of councils, opinions of ancient writers, doctrines of men, and private spirits, are to be examined, and in whose sentence we are to rest, can be no other but the Holy Spirit speaking in the Scripture." This drive to recover the original intent of the apostolic Scripture embraced various aspects of the life of the Christian and of the church, such as liturgy and polity, not only its confessional doctrine. A major preoccupation of all Reformation groups was the reform of worship. Although some of

them, notably the Anglicans in the *Book of Common Prayer* and
the Lutherans in the *Deutsche Messe* and its various vernacular
successors, retained substantial portions of the medieval order of
the mass while excising those elements, such as invocation of the
Virgin Mary and of the other saints as well as prayers for the
departed, that they deemed inconsistent with biblical teaching,
others were far more radical in rejecting not only the Roman
Catholic mass but the "devised, imposed, stinted popish liturgy"
of the *Book of Common Prayer*, and in recasting their liturgies to
bring them closer to original and apostolic simplicity. In the celebration of the Lord's Supper, where in both East and West the
church had developed ever more elaborate rituals, as another
sixteenth-century confession put it, "We think that rite, manner,
or form of the supper to be *the most simple* and excellent which
comes nearest to *the first institution* of the Lord and to the apostles' doctrine"; but "to have public prayer in the church, or to
administer the sacraments in a tongue not understood of the people, is a thing plainly repugnant to the word of God *and the
custom of the primitive church.*" And in the organization of the
church, where the early rise of the monarchical episcopate had
grown into the patriarchal and papal systems of polity of Eastern
Orthodoxy and Western Catholicism, the title of the confession
of the General Baptists, issued in 1651, emphasized that they were
"gathered according to *the primitive pattern*"; and the confession
of the Mormons, issued in 1842, affirmed: "We believe in the
same organization that existed in *the primitive church.*" Upon
hearing a local clergyman "spoken of as an apostolic man,"
George Eliot's Dorothea Brooke Casaubon "was wishing it were
possible to restore the times of *primitive zeal.*"

Yet in the event, that affirmation of *sola Scriptura* in principle
was accompanied, in Luther and even in Zwingli and even in the
Anabaptists, by the retention in practice of a substantial piece of

the creedal and dogmatic tradition. But later Protestants in the eighteenth and nineteenth centuries, claiming to be carrying out for various doctrines a radical intention that the Reformers of the sixteenth century had been unable to accomplish, sought to be more consistent than they had been in pressing for the original intent of the New Testament over against the later creeds and liturgies. Even when he formulated some *Propositions* to explain his originalist position, therefore, Thomas Campbell warned: "Let none imagine that the subjoined propositions are at all intended as an overture towards a new creed, or standard, for the church. . . . They are merely designed for opening up the way, that we may come fairly and firmly to *original ground* upon clear and certain premises and take up things *just as the apostles left them.* . . . *disentangled from the accruing embarrassment of intervening ages.*"

"Come firmly to original ground, take up things just as the [framers] left them, disentangled from the accruing embarrassment of intervening ages": with the change of only one word, from "apostles" to "framers," Campbell's motto would summarize equally well the originalist impulse as applied to the Constitution. In claiming the right to overrule actions of individual states, for example, the Supreme Court had declared in 1859: "It was felt by the statesmen who framed the Constitution, and by the people who adopted it, that it was necessary that many of the rights of sovereignty which the States then possessed should be ceded to the General Government." And from the historical fact that "many of the members of the [Constitutional] Convention were also members of this [first] Congress" it concluded that "it cannot be supposed that they did not understand the meaning and intention of the great instrument which they had so anxiously and deliberately considered, clause by clause, and assisted to

frame." These framers had, after all, been the precise constitutional counterparts to the ones whom the New Testament identified as "those who from the beginning were eyewitnesses" (Lk
1.2).

William Paterson of New Jersey (1745–1806) was in the special position of being both a framer and an associate justice, as
well as one of the drafters of the First Amendment. Therefore,
while acknowledging that in the provision of the Constitution,
"The Congress shall have power to lay and collect taxes, duties,
imports, and excises" (art. 1, sec. 8), "what is the natural and
common, or technical and appropriate, meaning of the words,
'duty' and 'excise,' is not easy to ascertain," so that "they present
no clear and precise idea to the mind [and] different persons will
annex different significations to the terms," Justice Paterson felt
qualified by this special position of his to continue: "It was, however, *obviously the intention of the framers of the Constitution,* that
Congress should possess full power over every species of taxable
property, except exports. The term taxes, is generical, and was
made use of to vest in Congress plenary authority in all cases of
taxation. The general division of taxes is into direct and indirect.
Although the latter term is not to be found in the Constitution,
yet the former necessarily implies it." Again, two years later, with
a similar prefatory acknowledgment that a "usage makes up part
of the Constitution of Connecticut, and we are bound to consider
it as such, unless it be inconsistent with the Constitution of the
United States," Justice Paterson quoted the words of the Constitution of the United States, "that no state shall . . . pass any
bill of attainder, *ex post facto* law, or law impairing the obligation
of contracts" (art. 1, sec. 10); and, once more employing the word
"obvious," he invoked the special authority of the framers, even
when this contradicted his own moral and legal beliefs:

It is obvious from the specification of contracts in the last member of the clause, that the framers of the Constitution, did not understand or use the words in the sense contended for on the part of the Plaintiffs in Error. They understood and used the words in their known and appropriate signification, as referring to crimes, pains, and penalties and no further. The arrangement of the distinct members of this section, necessarily points to this meaning.

I had an ardent desire to have extended the provision in the Constitution to retrospective laws in general. There is neither policy nor safety in such laws; and, therefore, I have always had a strong aversion against them. . . . But on full consideration, I am convinced, that ex post facto laws must be limited in the manner already expressed; they must be taken in their technical, which is also their common and general, acceptation, and are not to be understood in their literal sense.

A special resource of "eyewitness" authority that has been available to those who inquire after the original intent of the framers of the Constitution is *The Federalist*. In one decision of the Supreme Court after another, therefore, the justices have gone to this source. To cite only one of the most important, the unanimous opinion of the Court in *Marbury* v. *Madison,* that "the particular phraseology of the constitution of the United States confirms and strengthens the principle, supposed to be essential to all written constitutions, that a law repugnant to the constitution is void; and that courts, as well as other departments, are bound by that instrument," found support in the original intent of the framers, as this had been formulated by Alexander Hamilton in *Federalist* 78:

There is no position which depends on clearer principles, than that every act of a delegated authority, contrary to the tenor of the commission under which it is exercised, is void. No legislative act therefore contrary to the constitution can be valid. . . .

It is not otherwise to be supposed that the constitution could intend to enable the representatives of the people to substitute their *will* to that of their constituents. . . . The interpretation of the laws is the proper and peculiar province of the courts. A constitution is in fact, and must be, regarded by the judges as a fundamental law. It therefore belongs to them to ascertain its meaning.

As the pseudonymous titles of *The Apostles' Creed*, the *Didache* or "Teaching of the Twelve Apostles," the fourth-century *Apostolic Constitutions*, the sixth-century *Corpus Areopagiticum* fathered on the shadowy Dionysius the Areopagite, whom Paul converted in Athens (Acts 17.34), and the "Apostolic Fathers" all show, there was a perceived need for an authentic parallel to *The Federalist* in the written sources of early Christianity, as distinct at any rate from the "unwritten traditions which were received by the apostles from the mouth of Christ himself, or else have come down to us, handed on as it were from the apostles themselves at the inspiration of the Holy Spirit," which were said to be reflected in later documents.

Justice Owen Josephus Roberts once posited the originalist position in a rather simplistic formula that echoes many definitions of the doctrine of the authority of Scripture in Protestant confessions: "When an act of Congress is appropriately challenged in the courts as not conforming to the constitutional mandate the judicial branch of the Government has only one duty,—to lay the article of the Constitution which is invoked beside the statute which is challenged and to decide whether the latter squares with the former." But the case against the arbitrary exercise of judicial power at the expense of the text of the Constitution can also be put in a far more nuanced way:

> Judges, who serve on good behavior, which typically means for life, can nullify the decision of elected officials, even though they themselves are not elected. If the power of judges is to be legitimated, they cannot be just another political organ of government. As they cannot appeal to popular will, they must be able to provide authoritative interpretations of the constitutional text that are not simply manifestations of their own private beliefs about what legislation should accomplish. In order for judges to make principled interpretations, the language of the Constitution must be clear and precise enough to bind even those who disagree with what it says, for the mission of constitutional government must soon founder if judges can decide cases as freely with the Constitution in place as without it.

In *The Wittenberg Articles* of 1536, Anglicans and Lutherans declared jointly: "We confess simply and clearly, without any ambiguity, that we believe, hold, teach, and defend everything which is in the canon of the Bible and in the three creeds, i.e. the Apostles', Nicene, and Athanasian Creeds, *in the same meaning which the creeds themselves intend and in which the approved holy fathers use and defend them.*" Similarly, a twentieth-century interpreter stated the principle and procedure for the interpretation of the confessions of the sixteenth century: "We are to understand and confess the Symbols in their original historic sense—that is, in the sense which the words and terms had when the documents in question were formulated, and not in the sense which some of the words and terms may subsequently have acquired through the dialectic of controversy. Thus we must not read into the Catholic Creeds as pre-Reformation documents the sense with which the Reformers may have invested certain of their terms."

An Interdisciplinary Approach

The need to interpret some sort of *Urkunde* or primary and original document asserts itself in so many areas of human thought and activity that it may be helpful to look at this problem also with an interdisciplinary approach. Of all the scholarly disciplines with which the interpretation of the Constitution, and of law generally, has been compared during the twentieth century, the one to which everyone is most indebted must certainly be literary theory. This could be documented from the frequency with which the names of Stanley E. Fish and Richard A. Posner—Fish coming from the study of English literature, Posner from jurisprudence—would appear in any citation index (if there were one) of articles and books on the subject, including this one. One of the most profound literary studies to deal with the specific theme of this chapter was an essay by William K. Wimsatt, Jr., on "the intentional fallacy," originally published in 1946. In it he expanded his earlier argument "that the design or intention of the author is neither available nor desirable as a standard for judging the success of a work of literary art" and "that this is a principle which goes deep into some differences in the history of critical attitudes." If the original intent of the poet is, in Wimsatt's words, "neither available nor desirable as a standard for judging," this implies both that the historian or literary biographer is not in a position to discern it by historical research, and that, even if this were not the case and the original intent were "available," the critic or judge or exegete should not invoke its authority in interpreting the text.

The second of Richard A. Posner's two conclusions about interpretation in law and in literary theory, as cited in the preceding chapter, is: "Interpretation is not much, and maybe not at all, improved by being made self-conscious, just as one doesn't become a better reader by studying linguistics." This conclusion may perhaps apply to some schools of literary theory, or so, at any rate, some critics have concluded. Even there, however, it *is* the case, as traditional philology has long maintained, that, certainly with texts in a foreign language and even with those in the vernacular, one truly does "become a better reader by studying" if not "linguistics," then at least grammar, and perhaps by consulting a reliable lexicon from time to time. This might prevent some of the egregious—and often hilarious—errors of interpretation that can result from understanding a word in a later sense that it could not have had originally. When *The Cambridge Platform,* published in 1648 by the same community of Massachusetts Congregationalists who had founded Harvard College in 1636 "for the training up of such in good literature, or learning, as may afterwards be called forth unto office of pastor or teacher in the church," defines the church as "a company of professors," or when two centuries later *The New Hampshire Confession* denounces "superficial professors," these confessions are referring not to members of a college faculty but to those who profess the true faith. Nevertheless, the dialogue between the interpretation of law and the interpretation of literature, for all the intriguing parallels that Posner's omnivorous reading has permitted him to draw all the way from Shakespeare to Dostoevsky to Kafka, may not be as decisive a test case as it has often been taken to be.

For in spite of the unquestionable historical clarification that studying law and literature in conjunction has sometimes brought to both fields, the interpretation of literature lacks a crucial dimension that is fundamental to the interpretation of law: the enforceably normative. In the salutary reminder of Owen Fiss, "a judicial interpretation is authoritative in the sense that it legitimates the use of force against those who refuse to accept or otherwise give effect to the meaning embodied in that interpretation," as well as because of "an ethical claim to obedience—a claim that an individual has a moral duty to obey a judicial interpretation." Both these conditions of authoritativeness apply to interpretations of the Bible by the church and to interpretations of the Constitution by the Supreme Court, but the first of them at any rate does not apply to interpretations of poetry or fiction by literary critics and scholars. Except perhaps for a book review by an offended colleague or a bad grade from an ideological professor, the wrong interpretation of a sonnet or a novel does not bring punishment upon the alleged perpetrator: it is neither a crime nor a sin. And that crucial dimension makes the interpretation of Holy Scripture a far more relevant and abiding analogue for the interpretation of law, and above all for the interpretation of the American Constitution, than literary theory is. Not for the duration of one trendy generation of literary critics (or one trendy generation of theologians), but from the very beginnings of the church, the interpretation of the Bible in fact *has* been "improved by being made self-conscious," for the very reason that it deals with the Great Code, as does the interpretation of law and *a fortiori* the interpretation of the Constitution.

Therefore another analogue from the arts and humanities that is in some ways closer to the interpretation of the Constitution, because of the normative role of the authority of the original, is the discipline of musical performance. It does entail the imperative that Fiss has called "an ethical claim to obedience—a claim that an individual has a moral duty to obey" the original of the musical score as it stands. Just as any inscription bearing a date identified as "B.C." would be an obvious forgery and not an original, the same would have to be true of any musical manuscript bearing the name of Johann Sebastian Bach that was scored for clarinet: it could not be an original by the composer. Yet judging on the basis of Mozart's enthusiasm upon discovering the clarinet, as this comes through in his letters and above all in his *Stadler Quintet* of September 1789 (Köchel 561), one can only imagine, with regret, how the composer of the oboe accompaniment for the tenor solo "Ich will bei meinem Jesu wachen" in the *Saint Matthew Passion* would have reveled in exploiting the tonal quality and timber of the clarinet. This is true especially because of Bach's sensitivity, in composing for the human voice, to what R. L. Marshall calls "the character of the text and the affective connotation associated in the period with particular instruments."

Now what, if anything, does this imply for the artistic "claim to obedience—a claim that an individual has a moral duty to obey" and the obligation of the present-day performer of Bach toward the original intent of the composer? May the performer introduce a clarinet, or substitute a concert grand piano for Bach's keyboard instruments, or mount a performance of the *Mass in B Minor* with a chorus of two hundred voices? As harpsichordist and Baroque scholar Ralph Kirkpatrick has noted, "the 'authentic' performance has a tendency to include the audience in an exercise of moral virtue that leads it to mistake boredom for edification." After a lifetime of conducting and interpreting most of the orchestral and operatic repertoire (he made his debut conducting *Die Walküre* at twenty-five), Erich Leinsdorf wrote a strong apologia describing himself—and any other conductor, and by extension any other performer—as "the composer's advocate," and

commending the restraint of "the type of personality that properly refuses to impose itself upon the music of Bach's time." By
contrast, in a famous review for the *New York Herald Tribune* of
a recital on a Steinway concert grand by Vladimir Horowitz at
Carnegie Hall on 6 March 1942, Virgil Thomson wrote: "If one
had never heard before the works Mr. Horowitz played last night
. . . or known others by the same authors, one might easily have
been convinced that Sebastian Bach was a musician of the Leo-
pold Stokowski type, that Brahms was a sort of flippant Gershwin
who had worked in a high-class night club and that Chopin was
a gypsy violinist."

If we move the question of original intent from the music of
the Baroque to the music of the twentieth century, the resources
for answering it become greater, but the question also becomes
more complicated. Thus there have been, for example, several
recordings of Igor Stravinsky conducting his *Rite of Spring;* there
are also living memories of his doing so. It has been said that "of
all Stravinsky's works, *The Rite of Spring* is in every way the richest
in contrasts of every kind — contrasting rhythms, symmetrical and
asymmetrical, contrasts between heterogeneous harmonies, between melodies belonging to different tonal orbits, and between
utterly dissimilar tone-colors." But the "richness" of all these contrasts is underscored in the several readings of the score by the
composer himself, which sometimes differ in their tempi as well
as in their crescendos and "tone-colors." And this in spite of Stravinsky's opinion, as expressed in his memoirs, that "*Le Sacre* is
arduous but not difficult, and the *chef d'orchestre* is hardly more
than a mechanical agent, a time-beater who fires a pistol at the
beginning of each section but lets the music run by itself." Now
which of these readings of *Le Sacre* represents the composer's
original intent, and which is authoritative — and are these two the
same? Is it the reading he gave soonest after the composition,

when he remembered his intention, or one or another later reading that was the product of mature reflection during the years since that riotous night of 29 May 1913 in Paris—or should it be the one that comes out of the meticulous scholarly analysis of the score as carried out by later musicologists?

"Learning's Crabbed Text": The Critique of Originalism

Even in the noble simplicity of Justice Black's "confessional" formulation as quoted earlier, originalist doctrines of the *sensus literalis* in interpretation, whether biblical or constitutional, run the constant danger of substituting pedantry for living experience, as Robert Browning's grammarian had, even on his deathbed:

> "Time to taste life," another would have said,
>   "Up with the curtain!"
> This man said rather, "Actual life comes next?
>   Patience a moment!
> Grant I have mastered learning's crabbed text,
>   Still there's the comment.
> Let me know all!" . . .
> So, with the throttling hands of death at strife,
>   Ground he at grammar;
> Still, through the rattle, parts of speech were rife

They also run the danger of absolutizing the wrong original.

For in a thoughtful article entitled "The Original Understanding of Original Intent," which draws upon hermeneutical history as a whole rather than only upon the writings and debates of the framers of the Constitution, H. Jefferson Powell has sought to turn the tables on the advocates of "original intent" by arguing that "as understood by its late eighteenth and early nineteenth century proponents, the original intent relevant to constitutional discourse was not that of the framers, but rather that of the parties to the constitutional compact—the states as political entities." The judicial, as distinct from the scholarly, case against originalism as a hermeneutical principle was systematically articulated by Justice William J. Brennan in the *Abington* case of 1962 on school prayer. With only slight adaptation, his critiques could apply to the authority of original intent in the interpretation of Christian Scripture as well as of American Scripture:

> An awareness of history and an appreciation of the aims of the Founding Fathers do not always resolve concrete problems. . . . A too literal quest for the advice of the Founding Fathers upon the issues of these cases seems to me futile and misdirected for several reasons:
>
> First, on our precise problem the historical record is at best ambiguous, and statements can readily be found to support either side of the proposition. . . .
>
> Second, the structure of American education has greatly changed since the First Amendment was adopted. . . .
>
> Third, our religious composition makes us a vastly more diverse people than were our forefathers. . . .
>
> Fourth, the American experiment in free public education available to all children has been guided in large measure by the dramatic evolution of the religious diversity among the population which our public schools serve.

"Textual Support in the Constitutional Language": The Authority of the Original

The authority of "original intent" is a special problem in the Christian interpretation of the Old Testament. That problem begins already with the use of the Old Testament by the New. It is a constant theme of all four Gospels, and in a special sense of the Gospel of Matthew, to depict Jesus as the Messiah who had been promised to Israel, and therefore as the fulfillment of specific promises set down in the law and the prophets. Some of those "fulfillments" do have, in their context, a point of reference and therefore an "original intent" that can be identified within the history of Israel and therefore, in the words of *The Irish Articles,* a "proper relation to the times in which they were first uttered." One of the most striking instances of this is the use of a passage from the Book of Hosea about the Exodus, "When Israel was a child I loved him, and out of Egypt have I called my son" (Hos 11.1), as a proof text for "what the Lord had spoken by the prophet" about the flight of the Holy Family to Egypt (Mt 2.15).

So what is, for the Christian interpreter, the authentic original intent of these and other similar passages? The event that is usually counted—and celebrated—as the beginning of the Protestant Reformation, Martin Luther's posting of the Ninety-Five Theses on 31 October 1517, opens with an appeal from the current teaching and practice of the church to the original intent and *sensus literalis* of the Gospels: "That when our Lord Jesus Christ says, 'Repent' (Mt 4.17), he means that the total life is to be one of repentance," not that we are to go through the ritual of contrition, confession, and satisfaction, the three components of the medieval sacrament of penance. In announcing this proposition, Luther was grounding himself in the philological argument first propounded by Lorenzo Valla, and then developed by Erasmus,

that the Gospel imperative here, *metanoiete,* should not be translated, as in the Vulgate, "Paenitentiam facite [do penance]," but
"acquire a new mind [*nous*]," which was the original intent and
literal sense of the word in the Gospel's account of the preaching
of Jesus. Far more than the concept of "the private interpretation
of Scripture," with which the Reformation is often identified in
the popular mind, it was this return *ad fontes* and to the original,
grammatical meaning of Scripture that inspired Luther and the
other Reformers. It was also an emphasis that they had in common with Erasmus and the Renaissance, in spite of other profound differences. In that sense, Scripture had to be not interpreted but delivered from interpretations to speak for itself.
Therefore, for example, it was necessary to reject the medieval
doctrine of purgatory as (in the Elizabethan language of the Anglican *Thirty-Nine Articles*) "a fond thing vainly invented, and
grounded upon no warranty of Scripture, but rather repugnant
to the word of God," also because the biblical proof text for it,
which was still being used in the twentieth century, "It is a holy
and wholesome thought to pray for the dead that they may be
loosed from their sins" (2 Mc 12.46), came from Second Mac-
cabees in the Apocrypha, of which the same Anglican *Articles*
insisted that "yet doth [the church] not apply [these books] to
establish any doctrine."

Initially, the response to this originalism confirmed Martin
Luther in his position. For at the Leipzig Debate in 1519, his
opponent, Johannes Eck, piled up arguments from precedent,
from church fathers, councils, and canon law. To which Luther
replied that he and Saint Paul would together withstand them
all! But when at the Marburg Colloquy between Luther and Ulrich Zwingli in 1529, ten years later, the issue came to the original
intent of "This is my body" in the words of institution of the
Eucharist, it was the problem of the "literal sense" of Scripture

that divided the two Reformers, and eventually the two main branches of Protestantism, the Lutheran and the Reformed. Within Swiss Reformed Protestantism, the two main branches, the Zwinglian and the Calvinist, were united in their opposition to "those ridiculous interpreters who insist on what they call the precise literal sense of the solemn words of the supper—'This is my body, this is my blood.' For without question we hold that they are to be taken figuratively." On another sacrament, the sacrament of penance, the Council of Trent, too, weighed in on the side of "approving and accepting the literal and true meaning of those words of the Lord" that conferred on the apostles, and through them on the priesthood, the power to forgive sins.

For the authority of the original intent of the Constitution in finding "textual support in the constitutional language," a fundamental geographical reality proved to be a fundamental interpretive problem as well. Neither British precedent nor the original thirteen colonies that ratified the Constitution had faced the navigational questions created by the incorporation of the Great Lakes and of several large navigable rivers into the territorial limits of the United States. The Constitution provides: "The judicial power shall extend . . . to all cases of admiralty and maritime jurisdiction" (art. 3, sec. 2). On the presupposition that was to be enunciated a few years later by Chief Justice Roger Brooke Taney, that the United States had "borrow[ed] . . . our system of jurisprudence from the English law; and . . . adopted, in every other case, civil and criminal, its rules for the construction of statutes," this admiralty clause had been taken in 1825 to mean what it meant in English law, namely, jurisdiction over "service [that] was substantially performed, or to be performed, upon the sea, or upon waters within the ebb and flow of the tide." When this ruling was challenged, the Supreme Court ruled in 1852 that interpretation of what the Constitution meant by "maritime jurisdiction" was to depend instead upon "the navigable character of the water, and not upon the ebb and flow of the tide." But in dissent from that majority opinion, Justice Peter Vivian Daniel set down one of the classic formulations of the doctrine of original intent:

> It is admitted that by the decisions in England, the jurisdiction of the admiralty . . . was limited to the ebb and flow of the tide; and it is admitted that by the previous decisions of this court the like limitations were imposed on the jurisdiction of the admiralty in this country . . . ; yet now, without there having been engrafted any new provision on the Constitution, without the alteration of one letter of that instrument, designed to be the charter of all federal power, the jurisdiction of the admiralty is to be measured by miles, and by the extent of the territory which may have been subsequently acquired, ... that the Constitution may, nay must be altered by the same process, and must be enlarged not by amendment in the modes provided, but, according to the opinions of the judiciary, entertained upon their views of expediency and necessity. My opinions may be deemed to be contracted and antiquated. . . . I cannot construe the Constitution either by mere geographical considerations . . . , but must interpret it by my solemn convictions of the meaning of its terms, and by what is believed to have been the understanding of those by whom it has been formed.

Justice Daniel's phraseology, "the understanding of those by whom it has been formed," states in constitutional terms Thomas Campbell's appeal to "come fairly and firmly to original ground upon clear and certain premises and take up things just as the apostles left them. . . . disentangled from the accruing embarrassment of intervening ages." Another example of this issue from the history of constitutional interpretation is the application of the coinage clause, which will be discussed in the following chapter.

"Historical Philology" / "Sacred Philology"

Among all the writings of Greek and Roman antiquity — indeed, perhaps among all writings of any kind that have ever existed — the Greek New Testament stands out for the sheer number of manuscripts in which it has been preserved; counting codexes, papyri, lectionary texts, versions, and important ancient citations, these run into the thousands. As a result, many of the principles and methods of textual criticism as applied to the Greek and Latin classics — and then to later works — are a product of the work of Renaissance humanists such as Valla and Erasmus on the "sacred philology" of the biblical text. In addition,

> it remains one of the most momentous linguistic convergences in the entire history of the human mind and spirit that the New Testament happens to have been written in Greek — not in the Hebrew of Moses and the prophets, nor in the Aramaic of Jesus and his disciples, nor yet in the Latin of the imperium Romanum, but in the Greek of Socrates and Plato, or at any rate in a reasonably accurate facsimile thereof, disguised and even disfigured though this was in the Koine by the intervening centuries of Hellenistic usage.

Therefore the vocabulary of the New Testament stands in continuity with the Greek language as a total entity and does not make sense outside that context. In the Protestant Reformation, the ability to handle technical questions of text and vocabulary in "the Old Testament in Hebrew, . . . and the New Testament in Greek . . . , [which,] being immediately inspired by God, and by his singular care and providence kept pure in all ages, are therefore authentical" because they were original, came to be a required part of the training not only of biblical scholars for preparing their commentaries and lectures but of parish clergy for preparing their sermons.

The text of the Constitution, being officially printed in an *editio princeps,* is not subject to the same philological requirements, although the discovery of a parchment version does raise interesting questions about the capitalization and punctuation of the printed text. The same is true, though to a significantly lesser degree, of its vocabulary. Nevertheless, beginning already with the first Supreme Court, the justices have in a similar fashion seen themselves as exegetes of the constitutional text, charged with the responsibility of investigating its philology and parsing its grammar. Thus Chief Justice John Marshall, parsing the provision of the Constitution that "the Congress shall have power . . . to make all laws which shall be necessary and proper for carrying into execution the foregoing powers" (art. 1, sec. 8), put his exegesis into the context of a comprehensive theory of language and semantics, which would be applicable to the biblical no less than to the constitutional text:

> Such is the character of human language, that no word conveys to the mind, in all situations, one single definite idea; and nothing is more common than to use words in a figurative sense. Almost all compositions contain words, which, taken in a their rigorous sense, would convey a meaning different from that which is obviously

intended. It is essential to just construction, that many words which import something excessive, should be understood in a more mitigated sense—in that sense which common usage justifies. The word "necessary" is of this description. . . . This word, then, like others, is used in various senses; and, in its construction, the subject, the context, the intention of the person using them, are all to be taken into view.

Three years earlier, in 1816, Justice Story, while acknowledging that "the constitution unavoidably deals in general language," insisted that "the language of the [third] article is manifestly designed to be mandatory," because it reads: "The judicial power of the United States shall [not 'may'] be vested in one supreme court, and in such inferior courts as Congress may from time to time ordain and establish" (art. 3, sec. 1); and, he concluded, "the language, if imperative as to one part, is imperative as to all."

Both because of "the historical philology behind the Second Amendment" and because of continuing controversy over its interpretation, especially in the twentieth century, the Second Amendment has been a laboratory for such phrase-by-phrase exegesis: "A well regulated Militia, being necessary to the security of a free State, the right of the people to keep and bear Arms, shall not be infringed" (amend. 2). It has been observed that "there is less agreement, more misinformation, and less understanding of the right of citizens to keep and bear arms than on any other current controversial issue"; and, as has been noted earlier, the amendment has long been what biblical exegetes call a *crux interpretum,* for scholars and for justices of the Court. "The right . . . of 'bearing arms for a lawful purpose'. . . . is not a right granted by the Constitution. Neither is it in any manner dependent upon that instrument for its existence. The second amendment declares that it shall not be infringed; but this . . . means no more than that it shall not be infringed by Congress": quoting this opinion of Chief Justice Morrison Remick Waite from 1876, Justice William Burnham Woods explained in 1886 that "the amendment is a limitation only upon the power of Congress and the National government, and not upon that of the States." As Leonard Levy has pointed out, moreover, "The Second Amendment is the only provision of the Bill of Rights that has a preamble," opening with a construction—described by David C. Williams as "the purpose clause"—that sounds grammatically as though it were a translation from the ablative absolute of a Latin original. Does this "ablative absolute" imply that if and when the security of a free state does not any longer depend on a well-regulated militia of yeomen and "embattled farmers" to "fire the shot heard round the world" (Emerson), but relies instead on a standing army, or on conscripts, which does not seem to be the original intent of "a well regulated Militia," it becomes permissible to infringe the right of the people to keep and bear arms? Also, because "in 1789, when used without any qualifying adjective, 'the militia' referred to all citizens capable of bearing arms," so that "the 'militia' is identical to 'the people,'" that raises the question whether "people" is to be taken to refer to individuals or to a collectivity, or whether it may even be translated (and interpreted) by Williams as "the Body of the People." The Fourth Amendment protects "the right of *the people* to be secure in their persons, houses, papers, and effects" (amend. 4); as Sanford Levinson observes, "it is difficult to know how one might plausibly read the Fourth Amendment as other than a protection of individual rights." On the other hand, "we the people" in the preamble to the Constitution does not appear to mean individuals, one by one.

Justice John Marshall Harlan, dissenting in the *Civil Rights Cases* of 1883, set forth a tantalizing blend of the case for original "intent" and the case for "internal sense":

> The opinion in these cases proceeds, it seems to me, upon grounds entirely too narrow and artificial. I cannot resist the conclusion that the substance and spirit of the recent amendments of the Constitution have been sacrificed by a subtle and ingenious verbal criticism. "It is not the words of the law but the internal sense of it that makes the law: the letter of the law is the body; the sense and reason of the law is the soul." . . . By this I do not mean that the determination of these cases should have been materially controlled by considerations of mere expediency or policy. I mean only, in this form, to express an earnest conviction that the court has departed from the familiar rule requiring, in the interpretation of constitutional provisions, that full effect be given to the intent with which they were adopted.

"Authorized Versions" as Authoritative Interpretations

There is probably no clearer instance of the imperative to respect the authority of the original, and even to discern the original intent, of any text—legal, biblical, or literary—than the assignment of translating it; nor is there any clearer instance of how difficult an assignment this is. The Italian proverb "Traduttore traditore [The translator is a traitor]" illustrates the difficulty or even impossibility of living up to the imperative completely. Another way to state the problem, and one that has special relevance here, is to rephrase the proverb to read "The translator is an _interpreter_" — which is, of course, the meaning of the word "interpreter" in common usage, as when in a broadcast interview someone is speaking a foreign language but the English-speaking audience hears "the voice of the interpreter," or when the English translation of a Reformation confession, paraphrasing the instruction of the apostle Paul (1 Cor 14.27), cites it as an acceptable rule "that no one should speak with tongues in the congregation without an interpreter."

But one of the most far-reaching historical and cultural differences between the Bible and the Constitution is not only that the Bible was written over many more centuries but also that it has stood, and has been interpreted, over many more, and in a great many more cultures and languages. From that perspective, American Scripture, now two hundred years old, is still a relatively recent interpretive experiment, compared with Christian Scripture at ten times that age. And although the American Constitution served as a model for other constitutions in newly established democracies during the twentieth century and will probably continue to do so in the twenty-first, that process has not necessitated the production of official translations of the Constitution of the United States into other languages for American citizens. Unlike its neighbor to the north, the United States has not legally declared itself a bilingual nation, in which official documents, including the Constitution, would be required to appear in both languages. To the contrary, as Justice Holmes opined in 1923, "if there are sections in the State where a child would hear only Polish or French or German spoken at home I am not prepared to say that it is unreasonable [or, therefore, unconstitutional] to provide [by state law] that in his early years he shall hear and speak _only English_ at school." But, in keeping with "the fundamental theory of liberty" it had articulated in 1925, which

"excludes any general power of the State to standardize its children by forcing them to accept instruction from public teachers
only," the Supreme Court in 1966 ruled not only that the Federal
Voting Rights Acts of 1965 was constitutional in itself but that it
overrode "the New York English literacy requirement [, which]
cannot be enforced to the extent that it is inconsistent with" that
act; therefore those citizens of New York who, as products of a
Puerto Rican schooling, were literate only in Spanish could not
be denied the franchise. Might it not be seen to follow eventually
from that decision, as a logical extension or perhaps even as a
constitutional right, that such voters should have an authorized
Spanish translation of the Constitution in order to be able to
exercise the franchise responsibly? Then the translators would
have to face a host of interpretive questions, because interpretation and translation are inseparable. They would have to make
their decisions "anxiously and deliberately . . . clause by clause."
But the translation of the Bible, largely because of the work of
Christian missions, has been a major force in the history of languages, sometimes being responsible for the first reduction of a
language to written form; therefore "much of the Western theory
and practice of translation stems immediately from the need to
disseminate the Gospels, to speak holy writ in other tongues."

Accordingly, as the confessions of the Protestant Reformation make clear, there is often a one-to-one historical correlation
between those who have elevated the authority of the original
intent of *sola Scriptura* over the tradition of the church (the original intent being, of course, most fully and faithfully preserved in
the original Hebrew and Greek), those who have urged or de-
manded that the worship of the church be in the language of the
people, and those who have insisted that "the Scriptures ought
to be translated out of the original tongues into all languages for

the common use of all men" — or, more poetically, in a recent confession bearing the title *Our Song of Hope,* that

> The Spirit has inspired Hebrew and Greek words,
> setting God's truth in human language,
> placing God's teaching in ancient cultures,
> proclaiming the gospel in the history of the world.
> The Spirit speaks truly what the nations must know,
> translating God's word into modern languages,
> impressing it on human hearts and cultures.

By the end of the twentieth century, the number of such languages had exceeded two thousand. But it has frequently been noted, sometimes with a certain irony, that the biblical "original" for which some of these advocates of original intent seem to be contending, especially in English-speaking Protestantism, is in fact not the Hebrew or Greek original at all but a translation, in their case the Authorized (or King James) Version of 1611, and that sometimes their defense of the "original" is based on a translation, or a mistranslation, that is distinctive to that version. To cite a seemingly trivial but highly revealing example: A nineteenth-century Protestant confession that opens its first article with the words, "We believe that the Holy Bible was written by men divinely inspired," goes on in its second article to confess: "We believe that there is one, and only one, living and true God, . . . whose name is Jehovah." As its biblical authority for this statement, the confession cites this passage in the Psalms from the Authorized (King James) Version: "Thou, whose name alone is Jehovah, art the most high over all the earth" (Ps 83.18 AV). But the name "Jehovah" is not in fact the name that was "written by men divinely inspired" in the Bible; rather, "when vowel

points were put into Hebrew MSS, those of 'Adonai' ['Lord']
were inserted into the letters of the Tetragrammaton, and since
the 16th cent[ury] the bastard word 'Jehovah,' obtained by fusing
the vowels of one word with the consonants of the other, has
become established," as though it were the original intent of the
Psalmist and of the Holy Spirit.

An illuminating sidelight on just how "authorized" the Authorized Version can be is furnished by the factual report of the
Supreme Court that, in the contested case of required Bible reading in Pennsylvania schools, "the student reading the verses from
the Bible may select the passages and read from any version he
chooses, although the only copies furnished by the school are the
King James version, copies of which were circulated to each
teacher by the school district." The principal rival to the "King
James Version" as a version authorized for reading in the Pennsylvania schools was the Douai-Reims Bible, which, being a translation from the Latin Vulgate rather than from the Hebrew and
Greek originals, was preferred by Roman Catholic students, while
Jewish students found objectionable any so-called Bible, regard-
less of translation, that included the books that Christians call the
New Testament.

Even more than the English Authorized Version, two earlier
translations of the Bible have been "authorized" in a special sense:
the Greek Septuagint and the Latin Vulgate. As the work of Jewish translators in Alexandria a century or so before the Common
Era, the Septuagint by its renderings of Hebrew into Greek provides data about how the text of the Old Testament was being
read and understood in at least that part of the Diaspora. In some
cases it reflects a vocalization of the consonantal text that differs
from the standardized vowel points that were put down in writing by the Masoretes several centuries later (on the basis of an
existing oral tradition): in Psalm 110.3, for example, the initial

Hebrew consonant is pointed in the Masoretic text with a qāmats to read ʿammᵉkhā, "your people"; but the Septuagint (followed by the Vulgate's *tecum*), with its reading *meta sou,* "with you," indicates a Hebrew original ʿimmᵉkhā. Which reading of the Hebrew should be taken to be the original or *Urtext?* For Christians, the answer to that question about the original is complicated by the special standing of the Septuagint. With some few notable exceptions, the quotations from the Old Testament in the New are Septuagint translations, even when the Greek has changed the "original intent" of the Hebrew. For the writers of the New Testament, who with the exception of Luke the Greek were all, according to tradition, Greek-speaking Jews, this Greek version of the Old Testament was their Scripture, and therefore it is to the translations in the Septuagint, not to the Hebrew original, that these New Testament writers refer. The "sign" promised in Isaiah, that "a young woman [*alma*] shall conceive and bear a son, and call his name Emanuel" (Is 7.14), where the Hebrew word *alma* leaves the status of the young women unspecified, is translated in the Septuagint with "a virgin [*parthenos*] shall conceive in the womb" (Is 7.14 LXX); and that is the translation quoted in the New Testament in support of the virginal conception of Jesus from Mary (Mt 2.22–23). Again, although the Greek word *angelos* can mean a messenger of any kind, also in biblical Greek (Gn 32.4 LXX; 1 Mc 1.44 LXX; Lk 7.24), the Septuagint translation of the Psalm verse "Who makest the winds thy messengers" (Ps 104.4 RSV) as "Who makes his angels spirits, and his ministers a flaming fire" (Ps 104.4 LXX) is sanctioned both by the New Testament (Heb 1.7) and by Christian liturgies; and the word "angels" refers to "the heavenly powers" in their nine ranks, as they had been described in the *Celestial Hierarchy* of Pseudo-Dionysius the Areopagite. For Eastern Orthodoxy, therefore, the authority of the Old Testament is the authority of the Septuagint, and the "original intent" of the Old Testament is the one reflected in the Greek translation, which it regards as "a true and perfect version" inspired by the same Holy Spirit as the Hebrew text itself.

The status of the Latin translation is in some ways similar, though even more complex. In reaction to the insistence of the Protestant Reformation on "the Old Testament in Hebrew, . . . and the New Testament in Greek," the fourth session of the Council of Trent granted authoritative status instead to "these entire books and all their parts as they have, by established custom, been read in the Catholic Church, and *as contained in the old Latin Vulgate edition.*" In the apologetic and defensive atmosphere of the First Vatican Council, it appeared necessary to reassert this teaching that "the complete books of the Old and the New Testament with all their parts, as they are listed in the decree of the said council *and as they are found in the old Latin Vulgate edition,* are to be received as sacred and canonical." To this the opponents of the First Vatican Council replied that "no translation of Holy Scripture can claim an authority superior to that of the original text." By the time of the Second Vatican Council, and after the issuance of the epoch-making encyclical of Pope Pius XII in 1943, *Divino afflante Spiritu,* the Roman Catholic Church, while continuing to give honorable mention to "the ancient translation of the Old Testament called the Septuagint" and to "that known as the Vulgate," stressed the authority of "the *original texts* of the sacred books" and urged that "if the interpreter of Holy Scripture is to understand what God has wished to communicate to us, he must carefully investigate what meaning the biblical writers *actually had in mind;* that will also be what God chose to manifest through their words."

Development of Doctrine
Patterns and Criteria

A teacher of the law can produce from his store both the new and the old (Mt 13.52 NEB)

"An Inner Dimension of Tradition"

Both the history of the American Republic and the history of the Christian Church make it clear that, alongside the authority of their original charters and in continuous interaction with that authority, the ongoing and cumulative interpretations of the Great Code in the form of tradition and precedent have come to occupy a privileged position of authority in their own right. The polemic of a fifth-century Western confession by Pope Leo the Great affirms this relation between the two: "A man who has not the most elementary understanding even of the creed itself can have learned nothing from the sacred texts of the New and Old Testaments. . . . At least he should have listened carefully and accepted the common and undivided creed by which the whole body of the faithful confess, . . . the purest source of the Christian faith." Almost exactly a century later, an Eastern confession by Emperor Justinian the Great summarized its position: "This is the sound tradition that we preserve, which we have received from the holy fathers. . . . This we would take as our companion during our life that we might be made citizens [of heaven]." As a result of this ascription of authority to the tradition of the church fathers, the words in which the apostle Paul claimed divine inspiration for the words spoken and written by himself and the other apostles, "We impart this in words not taught by human wisdom but taught by the Spirit" (1 Cor 2.13), could be taken to refer to "words taught by the Holy Spirit, that is, *the divinely inspired theological writings of the fathers.*" And therefore, in response to the Protestant insistence on *sola Scriptura,* the Council of Trent codified the correlation in this way: "Following the example of the orthodox fathers, the council accepts and venerates with a like feeling of piety and reverence [*pari pietatis affectu*] all the books of both the Old and the New Testament, since the one God is the author of both, as well as the traditions concerning both faith and conduct, as either directly spoken by Christ or dictated by the Holy Spirit, which have been preserved in unbroken sequence in the Catholic Church." It is instructive to trace this correlation through the legislation of the early ecumenical councils of the church.

Adopting a formula of the New Testament (1 Cor 15.3–4) about the Old Testament, the Second Ecumenical Council, which was the First Council of Constantinople in 381, expanded the creed originally set down by the First Ecumenical Council, the Council of Nicaea in 325, to confess that Christ "rose up on the third day *in accordance with the Scriptures.*" The Third Ecumenical Council, the Council of Ephesus in 431, adopted its statement of faith "not by way of addition but in the manner of a full statement, even as we have received and possess it from of old *from*

the Holy Scriptures and from the tradition of the holy fathers." The
Fourth Ecumenical Council, the Council of Chalcedon in 451,
concluded its definition of faith about the one person and the
two natures of Jesus Christ with an appeal to a multiple authority: "just as the [Old Testament] prophets taught from the beginning about him, and as [in the Gospels of the New Testament]
the Lord Jesus Christ himself instructed us, and as the creed of
the fathers [the tradition of the Councils of Nicaea and Constan-
tinople] handed it down to us." The Fifth Ecumenical Council,
the Second Council of Constantinople in 553, similarly concluded
with an appeal jointly to Scripture and to tradition, including the
tradition of its predecessor councils: "Such then are the assertions
we confess. We have received them from Holy Scripture, from
the teaching of the holy fathers, and from the definitions about
one and the same faith made by the aforesaid holy councils." The
Sixth Ecumenical Council, the Third Council of Constantinople
in 680–81, declared that it was "following without deviation in a
straight path after the holy and accepted fathers [and that it]
piously accorded in all things with the five holy and universal
councils," to which "this holy and universal council of ours has
also, in its turn, under God's inspiration [*theopneustōs*], set its
seal," therefore employing for itself (and for the other orthodox
councils and traditions) the technical New Testament term for
divine inspiration (2 Tm 3.16) that had originally been applied to
the Old Testament Scriptures. And the Seventh Ecumenical
Council, the Second Council of Nicaea in 787, declared its purpose to be "that the divinely inspired tradition of the catholic
church should receive confirmation by a public decree," anathe-
matizing "anyone [who] rejects any written or unwritten tradition of the church."

But such asseverations of continuity would seem to bear a
rather paradoxical relation to the realities of historical change.

According to John Henry Newman, when the Virgin Mary was named Theotokos by the Council of Ephesus in 431, this was "an addition, *greater perhaps than any before or since,* to the letter of the primitive faith"—although that council itself made a special point of explaining that this was not an addition [*prosthēkē*] but an amplification [*plērophoria*]. Or when the Second Council of Nicaea in 787 invoked the authority of "written or unwritten tradition of the church" to support the use of images in Christian worship, it had to confront all the contrary evidence, from the authority of written tradition at any rate, that seemed to come down on the side of rejecting images. Recognizing the complexity of this problem of continuity and change, as it pertains to the Constitution no less than it does to the Bible, Chief Justice John Marshall argued "not only from the nature of the instrument, but from the language" that "it is a *constitution* we are expounding," not "the prolixity of a legal code." He took this to mean that "only its great outlines should be marked, its important objects designated, and the minor ingredients which compose those objects, be deduced from the nature of the objects themselves." More than a century later, quoting this "memorable warning" of his predecessor against "a narrow conception" of the Constitution, Chief Justice Charles Evans Hughes, in turn, took it to mean that "it is no answer . . . to insist that what the provision meant to the vision of that day it must mean to the vision of our time."

Conscious as it has always been of the weight of precedent as normative tradition, the Supreme Court has nevertheless from time to time recognized—and at times has even acknowledged openly—the innovative and unprecedented nature of some action or opinion. Justice Goldberg articulated the need for such acknowledgment in *New York Times Co.* v. *Sullivan,* when, speaking to his brethren on the Court, he urged: "We must recognize that we are writing upon a clean slate." "We are required in this case to determine *for the first time,*" Justice William Brennan said in the same case, speaking for the Court, "the extent to which the constitutional protections for speech and press limit a State's power to award damages in a libel action brought by a public official against critics of his official conduct." Just how portentous such an acknowledgment of innovation could be is evident from the foreshadowing of Justice Brennan's phrase "for the first time" in an earlier decision of the Court (which, it should be noted, was a reaffirmation of the *Dred Scott* decision): "These propositions are new in the jurisprudence of the United States, as well as of the States; and the supremacy of the State courts over the courts of the United States, in cases arising under the Constitution and laws of the United States, is now *for the first time* asserted and acted upon in the Supreme Court of a State."

"Growth" is something we watch with pride in our children and grandchildren, and yet "growth" is also another word for cancer. Therefore the only way for the Supreme Court or a church council to defend a growth as not malignant but benign has been to show that "an inner dimension of tradition," as Georges-Yves Congar has styled it, is in fact "the idea of development," for which John Henry Newman, "not that he was the only one . . . , was and remains to this day the *locus classicus.*" In 1845, while he was still an Anglican—technically, if not any longer in heart and mind, for his reception into the Roman Catholic Church would come while the book was in the press—Newman wrote *An Essay on the Development of Christian Doctrine.* One of its twentieth-century editors has said of it: "There are certain works in the history of theology of which we can say that after their appearance nothing was ever again quite the same. We can say this of Augustine's *De civitate Dei,* of the *Summa theologiae* of Aquinas, of Calvin's *Institutes.* The *Essay on Development* is a work of this order." Newman revised it quite heavily a third of a century later, producing in 1878 "the last print or reprint on which I shall ever be engaged"; it is this revised edition that is being cited here, also because it is the only version currently in print. But Newman's *Essay on Development* has also proved to be of use to the study of constitutional law. Therefore "development of doctrine" is no longer confined to the history of Christian doctrine, where it arose, but seems to have also established itself as a quasi-technical term in the study of the Constitution. Together with such a term as "evolving doctrine," it serves as a more "organic" metaphor to describe doctrinal change, which is also the function it performs for the history of Christian doctrine.

Development of doctrine (or something very much like it) is an empirically demonstrable fact of both the history of Christian Scripture and the history of American Scripture. This was how the fourth-century Greek church father Gregory of Nazianzus explained the phenomenon of change and progressive revelation, as it applied to the doctrine of the Trinity in comparison with the Levitical regulations:

> In the case by which I have illustrated it, the change is made by successive subtractions [for example, of circumcision and of the dietary regulations]; whereas here perfection is reached by additions. For the matter stands thus. The Old Testament proclaimed the Father openly, and the Son more obscurely. The New [Testament] manifested the Son, and suggested the deity of the Spirit. Now the Spirit himself dwells among us, and supplies us with a clearer demonstration of himself. For it was not safe, when the Godhead of the Father was not yet acknowledged, plainly to proclaim the Son; nor when that of the Son was not yet received to burden us further

(if I may use so bold an expression) with the Holy Ghost; . . . but that by gradual additions, and, as David says, "goings up" [Ps 83.6 LXX] and advances and progress from glory to glory [2 Cor 3.18], the light of the Trinity might shine upon the more illuminated. For this reason it was, I think, that he *gradually* came to dwell in the disciples, measuring himself out to them according to their capacity to receive him.

Truth was changeless in itself, but both its disclosure and its perception developed and were "gradual."

For the interpretation of the Constitution, Justice Oliver Wendell Holmes, Jr., used the terms "development" and "organism" to argue:

> When we are dealing with words that also are a constituent act, like the Constitution of the United States, we must realize that they have called into life a being the development of which could not have been foreseen completely by the most gifted of its begetters. It was enough for them to realize or to hope that they had created an organism; it has taken a century and has cost their successors much sweat and blood to prove that they created a nation. The case before us must be considered in the light of our whole experience and not merely in that of what was said a hundred years ago.

Yet he did immediately add a qualification that could be called "textualist," at least in an exclusionary sense: "The treaty in question does not contravene any prohibitory words to be found in the Constitution." Related to development of doctrine is the argument from experience, as Holmes's closing words indicate.

Thus, after quoting James Madison as "the leading spirit in the preparation of the First Amendment," Chief Justice Hughes, for the Court, added: "The fact that for approximately one hundred and fifty years there has been almost an entire absence of attempts to impose previous restraints upon publications relating to the malfeasance of public officers is significant of the deep-seated conviction that such restraints would violate constitutional right."

Whatever its "original intent" may have been, the saying of Jesus, "A teacher of the law can produce from his store both the new and the old" (Mt 13.52 NEB), has been said to "sum . . . up the whole ideal of Matthew the evangelist and may well have been a self-portrait." It has been used to describe—and to justify—the ongoing development of doctrine as a faithful interpretation of the original deposit in Scripture and even a faithful interpretation of the subsequent tradition, as in the *Declaration on Religious Freedom of the Second Vatican Council* of 1965, which defended its innovative affirmation of religious liberty by reference to "the sacred tradition and teaching of the church from which it continually draws new insights in harmony with the old."

"New Insights in Harmony with the Old"

When casting about for analogies to the development of doctrine, Newman sometimes cites mathematics, as when he tries the parallel that "doctrines [which develop] stand to principles [which do not develop], as the definitions to the axioms and postulates of mathematics," or that "in mathematical creations figures are formed on distinct formulae, which are the laws under which they are developed." A more profound consideration of this parallel, however, leads him to conclude that the proof of a doctrine, whether political or dogmatic, is after all not the same as the proof of a Euclidian theorem, but that, on the contrary, there never has been an idea "that throve and lasted, yet, like mathematical truth, incorporated nothing from external sources." By extension, not only the Euclidean theorem but the Aristotelian syllogism fails to measure up as an appropriate way of describing how doctrines "develop." Thomas Aquinas, for example, could use logic, specifically his standard distinction between the implicit and the explicit, to explain that "later councils do not formulate a creed differing from one more ancient, but, against emerging heresies, make explicit by added phrases what was implicit in the earlier creed." Therefore, when Newman proposes "logical sequence" as the fourth of his notes of faithful development, he means, as he explains near the end of the book, that there is a "progress of the mind from one judgment to another," which does not preclude but accompanies "the power of assimilation" that he has described in the third note. Similarly, in constitutional interpretation the interrelation among the three components, "text, tradition, and reason," has been proposed by Michael J. Perry as the basis for a valid theory and method.

But it is noteworthy that instead of mathematics or logic, some of the most telling observations in Newman's *Essay* deal instead with our theme of the similarities between theology and jurisprudence as venues for the development of doctrine. In expounding the first note, "preservation of its type," he speaks about "the variations which are consistent or not inconsistent with identity in political and religious developments." Moreover, one of his illustrations for this first note is: "Those magistrates are called 'corrupt,' who are guided in their judgments by love of lucre or respect of persons." He applies this note to the history of the period "when Rome changed from a Republic to an Empire": "it was a real alteration of polity, or what may be called a corruption; yet in appearance the change was small." Again, in expounding the sixth note, "conservative action upon its past," he supports it with the observation: "Blackstone supplies us with an instance in another subject-matter . . . when he observes that 'when society is once formed, government results of course, as necessary to preserve and to keep that society in order.' " And for the seventh and final note, he returns to this parallel: "Sober men are indisposed to change in civil matters, and fear reforms and innovations, lest, if they go a little too far, they should at once run on to some great calamities before a remedy can be applied."

In 1845, Newman proposed seven "distinctive tests between corruption and decay," "tests which are," in Owen Chadwick's phrase, "rather pegs on which to hang a *historical* thesis than solid supports for a doctrinal explanation": "preservation of type or idea; continuity of principles, power of assimilation; early anticipation; logical sequence; preservative additions; chronic continuance." In the revision of 1878, still with the intent "to discriminate healthy developments of an idea from its state of corruption and decay," he employed a slightly different order and phraseology, softening their force by calling them now not "tests" but only "notes," or even at one point "tokens": "preservation of its type; continuity of its principles; its power of assimilation; its logical sequence; anticipation of its future; conservative action upon its past; its chronic vigor." In a footnote Thomas C. Grey has called attention to these for their potential contribution to the relation between original intent and development of doctrine in the interpretation of the United States Constitution. The description by Edward H. Levi of developments in constitutional interpretation by the Supreme Court is sometimes even more true of developments in biblical interpretation by councils, synods, and confessions: "The development proceeds in shifts; occasionally there are abrupt changes in direction."

"First Note. Preservation of Its Type [Preservation of Type or Idea]"

Defining this first "note," Newman takes this to be a universally accepted criterion: "Every calling or office has its own type, which those who fill it are bound to maintain; and to deviate from the type in any material point is to relinquish the calling." He backs this up with examples from the history of the priesthood and of monasticism as well as, significantly, from the history of politics and jurisprudence. But he does add: "We cannot determine whether a professed development is truly such or not, without some further knowledge than an experience of the mere fact of this variation. Nor will our instinctive feelings serve as a criterion." "More subtle still and mysterious," he warned, "are the variations which are consistent or not inconsistent with identity in political and religious developments." Therefore "one cause of corruption in religion is the refusal to follow the course of doctrine as it moves on, and an obstinacy in the notions of the past."

Because it is so obvious as to seem self-evident — although in fact it is not — a prime case of the *preservation of its type* has been the *preservation,* across the spectrum of the creeds and confessions through the centuries, of binding "confession" and "doctrine," even of "dogma," and the insistence that "in a confession, accuracy [*akribeia*] in all respects is preserved and required." This was defined by the early church, above all in the creeds and decrees of the seven ecumenical councils between the First Council of Nicaea in 325 and the Second Council of Nicaea in 787. Although the Protestant Reformation represented a break with the continuity of the centuries in the very structure of the church, in its liturgy, in its ascetical life, and in many other fundamental respects, it is in the Protestant confessions of faith, more even than in the formularies of Roman Catholicism during that period, that this *type* of believing and confessing, or of interpreting Scripture and "making confession," or of "believing, teaching, and maintaining," is nevertheless especially *preserved*. *The First Helvetic Confession* in its German text employs the formula "we confess [*bekennen wir*]," for which the Latin is "we assert [*asserimus*]." *The French Confession* begins with "We believe and confess [*Nous croyons et confessons*]." *The Scots Confession* describes itself as "this brief and plain confession of that doctrine which is set before us, and which we believe and confess," and as "the confession of our faith, as in the following chapters"; and it proceeds to employ this phraseology throughout those following chapters: "We confess and acknowledge"; "We confess and believe"; "We believe and confess"; and "We affirm and avow." Its supplementary confession, *The King's Confession,* expands this phraseology to the full-blown "We believe with our hearts, confess with our mouths, subscribe with our hands, and constantly affirm before God and the whole world." *The Belgic Confession* opens with: "We all believe in our hearts and confess with our mouths." The first chapter of *The Second Helvetic Confession* begins with the words "We believe and confess [*Credimus et confitemur*]"; the third chapter begins with "We believe and teach"; and the eleventh chapter declares "We further believe and teach" and "We believe and teach." The Lutheran *Formula of Concord* repeatedly introduces its affirmations of various doctrines in successive articles with "We believe, teach, and confess."

The same *preservation of its type* of confession of doctrine is evident even in the Radical Reformation. The Anabaptist *Hans Denck's Confession Before the Council of Nuremberg* opens each article with the formula it employs at the beginning: "I, Hans Denck, confess"; and it concludes with the following coda: "All this I confess from the depth of my heart before the countenance of the invisible God, to whom through this confession I most humbly submit myself." Almost every article of a seventeenth-century Mennonite confession invokes some variant on the formula "We believe and confess, according to Scripture." Similarly, the confessions of nineteenth- and twentieth-century groups that arose outside the mainstream nevertheless *preserved* the traditional *type* of the creedal and confessional imperative. The confession entitled *The Statement of Belief of the Seventh-Day Adventist Church,* issued in 1872, goes beyond the conventional identification of that church with the doctrine of the second coming and the doctrine of the Sabbath to include the principal components of faith and confession. The Church of Christ, Scientist in its normative *Science and Health with a Key to the Scriptures* includes a statement with the heading: *Tenets of the Mother Church.* A few decades earlier, the Mormon Church issued *Articles of Faith of the Church of Jesus Christ of Latter-Day Saints,* and the Friends Yearly Meeting *The Richmond Declaration of Faith* for the Quakers. And in 1916 *The Statement of the Fundamental Truths of the Assemblies of God* declares the common doctrinal faith shared by the several Pentecostal groups making up that newly created denomination. After "avow[ing] our faith in God as Eternal and All-Conquering Love, in the spiritual leadership of Jesus," a Unitarian statement of faith concluded with the warning: "Neither this nor any other statement shall be imposed as a creedal test," but added the surprising codicil, "provided that the faith thus indicated be professed." *The United Church of Christ in Japan Confession of Faith* of 1954 introduces its reaffirmation of *The Apostles' Creed* with the formula: "Thus we believe, and with the saints in all ages we confess."

A *preservation of its type* of another sort is evident in the phrase "due process of law," a phrase that can also appear in a Christian confession as the English translation of the Latin *ordo iudiciorum.* The due process clause was not explicitly a part of the Constitution as such but was incorporated into the Bill of Rights: "nor [shall any person] be deprived of life, liberty, or property without due process of law" (amend. 5). With the passage of the Fourteenth Amendment, ratified in 1868, part of which read "nor shall any State deprive any person of life, liberty, or property, without due process of law" (amend. 14, sec. 1), it became, though not immediately and not without much controversy about "incorporation," a primary instrument for eventually extending to the state governments as well as the federal government the application of other constitutional provisions, and above all of the Bill of Rights in the first ten amendments, because "the one mass breakdown of our conventional form of criminal trial took place during the Civil War." Already before the outbreak of the Civil War and the passage of the Fourteenth Amendment, Justice Benjamin Robbins Curtis saw due process as a *preservation of a type or idea* from the English law, because, he said, "the words, 'due process of law,' were undoubtedly intended to convey the same meaning as the words, 'by the law of the land,' in *Magna Charta.*" With the Fourteenth Amendment, it was, as Chief Justice Charles Evans Hughes put it, "no longer open to doubt that the liberty of the press [originally protected from the federal government by the First Amendment] . . . is within the liberty safeguarded by the due process clause of the Fourteenth Amendment from invasion by state action," not only by federal action. In spite of Justice Felix Frankfurter's warning that "due process of law, 'itself a historical product,' is not to be turned into a destructive dogma against the States in the administration of their systems of criminal justice," the *preservation*—and, indeed, expansion—of this *type* went on to bring about, after a long period of relative inactivity, what has sometimes been described as a "due process revolution" in the twentieth century.

"Second Note. Continuity of Its Principles [Continuity of Principles]"

Because "doctrines expand variously according to the mind, individual or social, into which they are received," according to Newman, it is necessary to see that "the life of doctrines may be said to consist in the law or principle which they embody." Systems of philosophy, for example, "proceed upon the assumption of certain conditions which are necessary for every stage of their development . . . and the application of science to practical purposes depends upon the hypothesis that what happens today will happen tomorrow." Conversely, "the destruction of the special laws or principles of a development is its corruption." Therefore "doctrines develop, and principles at first sight do not; doctrines grow and are enlarged, principles are permanent. . . . Systems live in principles and represent doctrines"; hence "doctrines stand to principles, as the definitions to the axioms and postulates of mathematics." Later, as an explanation of this second note, he cites "a reference to Scripture throughout, and especially in its mystical sense." In sum, "When developments in Christianity are spoken of, it is sometimes supposed that they are deductions and diversions made at random, according to accident or the caprice of individuals; whereas it is because they have been conducted all along on definite and continuous principles that the type of the Religion has remained from first to last unalterable."

That quest for such "definite and continuous principles," of which, early in the history of the Supreme Court, Chief Justice John Marshall spoke as "*principles* which are common to our free institutions" that repose in—and yet in some sense stand beyond—"the particular provisions of the constitution of the United States," has been an ongoing preoccupation of the Supreme Court. In the third year of the Court's functioning, Justice

James Iredell felt constrained to articulate "the *general principles,* which influence me, on this point, succinctly and clearly." And, speaking through Justice Samuel Chase, the eighteenth-century Supreme Court strongly affirmed the criterion that Newman identified as *continuity of principles* in these words:

> This *fundamental principle* flows from the very nature of our free Republican governments, that no man should be compelled to do what the laws do not require; nor to refrain from acts which the laws permit. . . . There are certain *vital principles* in our free Republican governments, which will determine and over-rule an apparent and flagrant abuse of legislative power. . . . An act of the legislature (for I cannot call it a law), contrary to *the great first principles* of the social compact, cannot be considered a rightful exercise of legislative authority. . . . The *general principles* of law and reason forbid [certain acts of legislation].

This affirmation of Justice Chase would later serve as the basis for an argument by counsel before the Supreme Court that "the legislative power is restrained and limited by the *principles of natural justice.*"

In the nineteenth century this affirmation of *continuity of principles* and its use as an interpretive tool by the Supreme Court continued. "It is an established rule for the construction of statutes," Chief Justice Salmon Portland Chase asserted, "that the terms employed by the legislature are not to receive an interpretation which conflicts with *acknowledged principles of justice and equity,* if another sense, consonant with those *principles,* can be given to them." In 1886 the court identified it as a *"principle of interpretation* [that] has been sanctioned by this court" that "though the law itself be fair on its face and impartial in appearance, yet, if it is applied and administered by public authority with an evil eye and an unequal hand, so as practically to make unjust and illegal discriminations between persons in similar circumstances, material to their rights, the denial of equal justice is still within the prohibition of the Constitution."

It was still at work in the twentieth century, too:

> Time works changes, brings into existence new conditions and purposes. Therefore a *principle* to be vital must be capable of wider application than the mischief which gave it birth. This is peculiarly true of constitutions. They are not ephemeral enactments, designed to meet passing occasions. . . . In the application of a constitution, therefore, our contemplation cannot be only of what has been but of what may be. Under any other rule a constitution would indeed be as easy of application as it would be deficient in efficacy and power. Its *general principles* would have little value and be converted by precedent into impotent and lifeless formulas. Rights declared in words might be lost in reality.

In his famous dissent in *Lochner,* Justice Holmes appeared to be saying that "the natural outcome of a dominant opinion," which otherwise carried the presumption of credibility, could be resisted only when "it can be said that a rational and fair man necessarily would admit that the statute proposed would infringe *fundamental principles* as they have been understood by the traditions of our people and our law." Justice Benjamin Cardozo in 1937 declared that certain rights represented "the very essence of a scheme of ordered liberty, . . . *principles of justice* so rooted in the traditions and conscience of our people as to be ranked as fundamental." In 1952, Justice Felix Frankfurter insisted that decisions about restrictions on police power "are not sports in our constitutional law but applications of a *general principle*." And in 1963 Justice Hugo Black on that basis appealed from recent decisions of the Supreme Court, commending the Court because, as he put it, "in returning to these old precedents, sounder we believe than the new, we but restore *constitutional principles* established to achieve a fair system of justice." The following year Justice Brennan also voiced his view of principles, warning: "This Court's duty is not limited to *the elaboration of constitutional principles;* we must also in proper cases review the evidence to make certain that those *principles* have been constitutionally applied."

One of the central difficulties with which Newman's *Essay on Development* attempted to come to terms was that "the language of the Ante-nicene Fathers, on the subject of our Lord's Divinity, may be far more easily accommodated to the Arian hypothesis" than later orthodoxy. And so, if it is right to speak about a *principle* of biblical theology, as the term *principium* or *archē* was confessed by both the West and the East, that could not be a reference to anything except the *principle* of the monotheistic faith in the one true God: "In *principio* creavit Deus" (Gn 1.1 Vulg); "In *principio* erat Verbum" (Jn 1.1 Vulg). Liturgically as well as creedally, it is set down in the primal confession of *The Shema* (Dt 6.4): "Hear, O Israel: The Lord our God is one Lord." The New Testament quotes *The Shema* verbatim and in full only once (Mk 12.29); but there it is spoken by One who, in that same Gospel (Mk 1.11) and at many other places in the New Testament, was being addressed with divine titles, described with divine attributes, and credited with divine powers and acts. The fundamental interpretive dilemma was, therefore, how this person who was God could speak this way about the one God, and therefore how the confession of the church was to speak of the one God in such a way as to take full account of the unique relation between Jesus Christ and his Father. Or, in the lapidary formulation of this dilemma by Adolf Harnack, "Is the Divine that has appeared upon the earth and reunited man with God [and that quoted *The Shema*] identical with the supreme Divine who rules heaven and earth [as confessed in *The Shema* to be One], or is it a demigod?" The answer to that interpretive dilemma was the doctrine of the Trinity, in which it was the Nicene Trinitarians, not the Arians, who could claim to be the true unitarians, because the Arians continued to worship as a demigod one whom they denied to be true God in the full sense. Therefore the first official conciliar codification of the doctrine of the Trinity, in 325, opened with the Jewish *Shema* in a Christian creedal formulation: "We believe in one God." This was followed in the very same words a half-century later by the definitive creedal formulation of *The Shema* in *The Niceno-Constantinopolitan Creed,* which would become the most universal of all Christian statements of faith; this was, as the Eastern Orthodox liturgy put it, a confession of "the Trinity, one in essence and undivided," in which, as a later Protestant confession put it, "there is the Father, the Son, and the Spirit, being every one of them one and the same God, and therefore not divided, but distinguished one from another by their several properties." On the grounds of "getting rid of polytheism," the opponents of that creedal formulation used "the pretext of honor to one God not to believe at all in the true God." But once having been set down for all time to come in the trinitarian dogma, the trinitarian *principle* then became the underlying *principle* of christological dogma as well, so that councils, creeds, and confessions dealing with the dogma of the two natures in Christ, rather than with the dogma of the Trinity as such, nevertheless had to begin by affirming: "There is only one God." It would not do to speak about the relation between Father, Son, and Holy Spirit in the

Trinity in any fashion that smacked of "pagan multiplicity" and polytheism. For the same reason, the decree of the seventh ecumenical council in 787, validating the use of images in the liturgy of the church on the grounds that "it provides confirmation that the becoming man of the Word of God was real and not just imaginary," immediately hemmed itself in with the explanatory *principle* that "this is not the full adoration in accordance with our faith, which is properly paid only to the divine nature." But the relation of such *principles* to the exegesis of the authoritative text would also continue to be a source of controversy for both interpretive communities.

"Third Note. Its Power of Assimilation [Power of Assimilation]"

Taking growth in the natural world as his analogy for development of doctrine, Newman posits the thesis: "An eclectic, conservative, assimilating, healing, moulding process, a unitive power, is of the essence, and a third test, of a faithful development." For there has never been an idea "that throve and lasted, yet, like mathematical truth, incorporated nothing from external sources." And "the stronger and more living is an idea . . . the more able is it to dispense with safeguards, and trust to itself against the danger of corruption."

Newman has been quoted earlier as saying that the adoption of the title "Theotokos" for the Virgin Mary by the Council of Ephesus in 431 was "an addition, greater perhaps than any before or since, to the letter of the primitive faith." Coming as it did in the very city in which the missionary activity of the apostle Paul had evoked the fighting words of pagan goldsmiths, "Great is Artemis of the Ephesians!" (Acts 19.28), the legislation of this title could be interpreted—and has been—as the dogmatic codification of the words of Elizabeth to Mary in the Gospel of Luke (Lk 1.42–43): "Blessed are you among women, and blessed is the fruit of your womb! And why is this granted to me, that *the mother of my Lord* should come to me?" But it could also be interpreted—and has been—as the *assimilation* of the Ephesian cult of the mother goddess Diana-Artemis to the uses of the growing cult of Mary the Mother of God. Regardless of which of these two interpretations may be valid, the question still is: What is the difference, not only between benign and malignant growth in general but between valid and invalid *assimilation* of ideas, concepts, and titles, and which of these is at work in the adoption of the title "Mother of God"? The principle of *assimilation* was well summarized in a fourteenth-century Orthodox formula: "Let us grant that one of the heretics was the first to say this. It is no crime in us if we use well what they invented badly."

Employing this very word *assimilate,* Thurman Arnold formulated the issue trenchantly for the law and for the interpretation of the Constitution: "Science is recognized as a way of finding out the truth, so the law must find a rational place for science. Economics and sociology demand recognition. Psychology makes its claim. The law cannot ignore these ideas or these techniques. Neither can it *assimilate* them until they have been changed into rational principles." An influential instance of such *assimilation* from other disciplines was the "sociological jurisprudence" in the "very copious collection" of a brief containing "other than judicial sources" and filed by Louis D. Brandeis several years before his appointment to the Supreme Court. The controversial use and assimilation of empirical evidence about the functioning of juries formed the basis for far-reaching proposals of reform. But the problems faced in the *assimilation* of ideas from such "external sources" came into focus even more dramatically in two famous decisions of the Supreme Court in the twentieth century. In *Buck*

v. *Bell,* which dealt with the constitutionality of the compulsory sterilization of the mentally retarded, Justice Oliver Wendell Holmes, Jr., for the Court, *assimilated* from external sources the evidence "that heredity plays an important part in the transmission of insanity, imbecility, etc."; and then he continued, with an echo of his own searing battle experience during the Civil War: "We have seen more than once that the public welfare may call upon the best citizens for their lives. It would be strange if it could not call upon those who already sap the strength of the State for these lesser sacrifices, often not felt to be such by those concerned, in order to prevent our being swamped with incompetence. It is better for all the world, if instead of waiting to execute degenerate offspring for crime, or to let them starve for their imbecility, society can prevent those who are manifestly unfit from continuing their kind." And he concluded: "Three generations of imbeciles are enough."

In *Plessy* v. *Ferguson,* the Supreme Court had also *assimilated* "external sources" when it upheld the constitutionality of "separate but equal" facilities for the two races under the Fourteenth Amendment, on the grounds that "in determining the question of reasonableness [the state legislature] is at liberty to act with reference to the established usages, customs and traditions of the people, and with a view to the promotion of their comfort." Therefore it rejected, as an "underlying fallacy," the argument "that the enforced separation of the two races stamps the colored race with a badge of inferiority." Against that background, Justice Frank Murphy was speaking not only for himself but for others when in his dissent in *Korematsu* he criticized the Court's *assimilation* of "questionable racial and sociological grounds" to interpret the Constitution. Once more *assimilating* "racial and sociological grounds" and "external sources," but this time quite different ones and to a quite different conclusion, Chief Justice

Earl Warren in *Brown*, after quoting the opinion of the state court ("which nevertheless felt compelled to rule against the Negro plaintiffs") that "segregation of white and colored children in public schools has a detrimental effect upon the colored children," continued: "Whatever may have been the extent of psychological knowledge at the time of *Plessy* v. *Ferguson*, this finding [in *Brown*] is amply supported by modern authority"; and then in Footnote Eleven, which in the scholarly literature has since taken on a life of its own, he added seven references to social science research, citing sociologists and psychologists from Kenneth Clark to Gunnar Myrdal's *American Dilemma* of 1944.

"Fourth Note. Its Logical Sequence [Logical Sequence]"

Nevertheless, "such intellectual processes, as are carried on silently and spontaneously in the mind of a party or school, of necessity come to light at a later date, and are recognized, and their issues are scientifically arranged. And then logic has the further function of propagation; analogy, the nature of the case, antecedent probability, application of principles, congruity, expedience, being some of the methods of proof by which the development is continued from mind to mind and established in the faith of the community." "There is a certain continuous advance and determinate path which belong to the history of a doctrine, policy, or institution, and which impress upon the common sense of mankind, that what it ultimately becomes is the issue of what it was at first." Newman saw this as a process of "one doctrine leading to another; so that, if the former be admitted, the latter can hardly be denied, and the latter can hardly be called a corruption without taking exception to the former."

One of the most sustained linear processes of such *logical sequence* in the history of the interpretation of Christian Scripture by the church can be traced in the Christology of the Fourth, Fifth, and Sixth Ecumenical Councils, from the Council of Chalcedon in 451 through the Second Council of Constantinople in 553 to the Third Council of Constantinople in 680–81: not one but two natures in the one person of Jesus Christ (Chalcedon); therefore not one but two wills (Constantinople II); and therefore also not one but two principles of action or "energies" (Constantinople III). As a Western synod described this *logical sequence,* "As we confess that he truly has two natures or substances . . . , so also the rule of piety instructs us that he has two natural wills and two natural operations." This "rule of piety" could be corroborated by the rule of *logical sequence:* "What man *who thinks logically* will ever be able to demonstrate, when they say [nature or will or principle of action] is one, whether they can say it is temporal or eternal, divine or human, uncreated or created, the same as the Father's or different from the Father's? If (you see) it is one and the same, it is one and common to the divinity and humanity of Christ, which is absurd." In a formula that would survive into the creeds and confessions of the Protestant Reformation more than a millennium later, it was affirmed at Chalcedon in 451 to be orthodox teaching that "one and the same Christ [is to be] acknowledged in two natures which undergo no confusion, no change, no division, no separation [*asynchytōs, atreptōs, adiairetōs, achōristōs*]." Now "in accordance with this reasoning," those same four Greek exclusionary adverbs could likewise go on to describe the two wills, and then the two principles of action (energies), in Christ. As an interpretation of the Gospel story of Christ's raising of Lazarus (Jn 11.1–46), for example, this Chalcedonian doctrine of two natures—and, by this *logical* extension, of two wills and two principles of action— meant that "it does not belong to the same nature to weep out of deep-felt pity for a dear friend (Jn 11.35) [which was an act of the human nature of Christ], and to call him back to life again at the word of command (Jn 11.43) [which was an act of the divine nature of Christ]." But by an application of *logical sequence* it became a pattern of development that each nature, being complete, had to have a will and then that each nature had to have a principle of action. Therefore it was a key to interpretation that could explain the prayer of Jesus before his suffering and death, "Not my *will* [singular], but thine [singular], be done" (Lk 22.42) to mean "two natural volitions or wills in him," one divine and one human, and the all-but-apostolic formula attributed to Dionysius the Areopagite, "a single divine-human principle of action," to mean "two natural principles of action." And by a further *logical sequence,* the Seventh Ecumenical Council decreed against iconoclasm that "the production of representational art . . . provides confirmation that the becoming man of the Word of God was real and not just imaginary." Yet to a Reformed confession, this was not a *logical sequence* at all but an unwarranted stretch; for "although Christ assumed human nature, yet he did not on that account assume it in order to provide a model for carvers and painters." So ingrained was this principle of *logical sequence* in Christian interpretation, however, that it came to qualify Protestant definitions of *sola Scriptura,* to mean ascribing equal scriptural authority to what "is either expressly set down in Scripture, or by good and necessary consequence may be deduced from Scripture."

Among the many enunciations of the note of *logical sequence* in the history of constitutional interpretation, the formulation of Justice Tom Clark may serve: "Moreover, our holding that the exclusionary rule is an essential part of both the Fourth and the Fourteenth Amendments is not only *the logical dictate of prior cases,* but it also makes very good sense. There is no war between the

Constitution and common sense." It was a form of this note of *logical sequence* when, in *Marbury* v. *Madison,* the conclusion was based, not on this or that clause of the Constitution of the United States as such, but on "particular phraseology of the constitution of the United States," which *logically* "confirms and strengthens the principle, supposed to be essential to all written constitutions, that a law repugnant to the constitution is void; and that courts, as well as other departments, are bound by that instrument." Therefore, by the *logical sequence* of the methods either of deduction or of inference, a determination of the meaning of the Constitution had to include not only the powers it expressly spells out but also what "may be *deduced* fairly from more than one of the substantive powers expressly defined, or from them all combined. It is allowable to group together any number of them and *infer* from them all that the power claimed has been conferred."

"Fifth Note. Anticipation of Its Future [Early Anticipation]"

"Since developments are in great measure only aspects of the idea from which they proceed, and all of them are natural consequences of it," according to Newman, "it is often a matter of accident in what order they are carried out in individual minds. . . . The fact, then, of such early or recurring intimations of tendencies which afterwards are fully realized, is a sort of evidence that those later and more systematic fulfilments are only in accordance with the original idea." But a determination of just when it finally does become appropriate for such developments to be "fully realized" in these "later and more systematic fulfilments" has much to do with their legitimacy and their "reception," defined by Georges-Yves Congar as "the process by means of which a church (body) [or a court] truly takes over as its own a resolution that it did not originate as to its self, and acknowledges the measure it promulgates as a rule applicable to its own life. . . . It includes a degree of consent, and possibly of judgment, in which the life of a body is expressed which brings into play its own, original spiritual resources." In the language of the church, this determination about timing has acquired the name "definability"; in the language of the Supreme Court, "ripeness," or the more Latinate "justiciability." But as Newman had to acknowledge, such *anticipations* could be quite "vague and isolated." Both historically and substantively, therefore, it was essential to recognize, at least by hindsight, that the dialectical pattern of the *anticipation* and development has often been complex rather than unilinear and that it has taken place "in shifts": early *anticipation* of the course / tack to starboard / midcourse correction.

Hence a development can sometimes be seen as the reversal of an earlier reading of the authoritative text. The bishops of the Council of Chalcedon in 451 insisted that the action of the First Council of Constantinople of 381, adopting *The Niceno-Constantinopolitan Creed,* which amplified *The Creed of Nicaea* of 325, was "not introducing anything left out by their predecessors, but clarifying their ideas about the Holy Spirit by the use of scriptural testimonies against those who were trying to do away with his sovereignty." But they manifested no such protective and tender care for the Synod ("Robber Synod, *latrocinium Ephesinum*") of Ephesus in 449, whose dogmatic position they reversed.

Justice Stanley Forman Reed, while "not unmindful of the desirability of continuity of decision in constitutional questions," insisted that "when convinced of former error, this Court has never felt constrained to follow precedent. In constitutional questions, where correction depends upon amendment and not upon legislative action[,] this Court throughout its history has freely exercised its power to reexamine the basis of its constitutional decisions." One example among many of such a midcourse correction by the Supreme Court, after an interval similar in its brevity to that between Ephesus II of 449 and Chalcedon of 451, is especially notable because in it Justice Owen J. Roberts reversed his own earlier decision. In 1936 he had, speaking for the Court, ruled the Agricultural Act of 1933 unconstitutional; but in 1939 he declared it to be constitutional after all, again writing the opinion for the Court. Although the dialectical pattern of *early anticipation,* tack to starboard, and midcourse correction in the interpretation of the Constitution on civil rights and race relations that is represented by the history of nearly a century, from the *Dred Scott* decision of 1857 to *Brown* v. *Board of Education* of 1953, took much longer than the two-year interval between *Ephesus II* and *Chalcedon* or the three-year interval between *Butler* and *Mulford,* it has in fact proved to be durable. In a further tack to starboard two years after *Dred Scott,* the Court reaffirmed and even extended it: "It is proper to say that, in the judgment of this court, the act of Congress commonly called the fugitive slave law is, in all of its provisions, fully authorized by the Constitution of the United States." But the recognition of the need for a correction of course had gone far enough by 1896 for Justice John Marshall Harlan, in dissent from the Court on *Plessy* v. *Ferguson,* to warn: "In my opinion, the judgment this day rendered will, in time, prove to be quite as pernicious as the decision made by this tribunal in the *Dred Scott case.*" And in spite of predictions, *Brown* did in fact establish itself as an accepted and permanent part of the legal and political landscape, fulfilling the *early anticipations* of it in the Bill of Rights and the Fourteenth Amendment, "vague and isolated" though these may have seemed to be.

"Sixth Note. Conservative Action upon Its Past [Preservative Addition]"

"A corruption," Newman defined, "is a development in that very stage in which it ceases to illustrate, and begins to disturb, the acquisitions gained in its previous history." Conversely, "a true development, then, may be described as one which is conservative of the course of antecedent developments[,] being really those antecedents and something besides them: it is an addition which illustrates, not obscures, corroborates, not corrects, the body of thought from which it proceeds; and this is its characteristic as contrasted with a corruption." "Blackstone supplies us with an instance in another subject-matter, of a development which is justified by its utility, when he observes that 'when society is once formed, government results of course, as necessary to preserve and to keep that society in order.' "

In the eyes of its Western defenders, the Filioque clause, the controversial addition of the words "and from the Son" to the original conciliar language of *The Niceno-Constantinopolitan Creed* about the "proceeding" of the Holy Spirit from the Father and the most divisive of the dogmatic differences between East and West, was such a *preservative addition*. According to one of its first official formulations, by a Spanish synod in 675, "We believe also that the Holy Spirit, who is the third person in the Trinity, is God, one and equal with God the Father and the Son, of one substance, also of one nature; *that he is the Spirit of both, not, however, begotten nor created but proceeding from both*." The *addition* was intended to be *preservative,* because, as its opponents formulated the argument for its proponents, "we want the Holy Spirit also to take his being from the Son, so that we may show that the Son is consubstantial and of equal power with the Father." But to those Eastern Orthodox opponents, it represented an "excessive and pointless" interpolation that "would dare to introduce two causes in the Holy Trinity." It was "contrary to the memorable declaration of our Lord [Jn 15.26, 'who proceeds *from the Father*'] . . . and contrary to the universal confession of the catholic church as witnessed by the seven ecumenical councils," which had interdicted all addition, or diminution, or alteration, or variation. But to its Latin defenders, it was not adopted "with the intention of excluding the Father from being the source and principle of all deity," and therefore it "was licitly and reasonably added to the creed for the sake of declaring the truth and from imminent need."

A *preservative addition* in the interpretation of the Constitution — and a favorite illustration for critics of the doctrine of original intent — is the development of the meaning of the coinage clause. It came at least in part out of the experience of the colonies with the ambiguity of currency in relation to specie. But it also reflects an international phenomenon at the end of the eighteenth and beginning of the nineteenth century, as the discussion of the value of paper money in act 1 of part 2 of Goethe's *Faust* shows. As it stands, the coinage clause of the Constitution refers explicitly only to specie, not to paper money: "The Congress shall have power . . . to coin money, regulate the value thereof, and of foreign coin" (art. 1, sec. 8). In 1870 the Supreme Court acknowledged that a decade earlier, before the Civil War, "there was, confessedly, no lawful money of the United States, or money which could lawfully be tendered in payment of private debts, but gold and silver coin"; it acknowledged, moreover, that there was not "in the Constitution any express grant of legislative power to make any description of credit currency a legal tender in payment of debts." The opponents of paper money maintained, therefore, that in the language of the Constitution,

which gives Congress power "to coin money and regulate the value thereof, and of foreign coins," it must be
evident that Congress [*sic:* the Constitution?] referred
only to *metallic money* . . . [and that] upon looking at the
public history of the times (which this court has established as a proper guide to the construction of the Constitution), we find that in the history of the country there
was no period in which "money" was more distinctly
understood and meant to be hard money than the period
when the Constitution was framed and adopted.

From this they drew the constitutional conclusion, as formulated
for them by Justice William Strong in his response to them, "that
the clause which conferred upon Congress power 'to coin money,
regulate the value thereof, and of foreign coin,' contains an implication that nothing but that which is the subject of coinage,
nothing but the precious metals can ever be declared by law to
be money, or to have the uses of money."

The dilemma was phrased in a balanced question by the
Court:

It is not doubted that the power to establish a standard of value by which all other values may be measured,
or, in other words, to determine what shall be lawful
money and a legal tender, is in its nature, and of necessity, a governmental power. It is in all countries exercised
by the government. In the United States, so far as it
relates to the precious metals, it is vested in Congress by
the grant of the power to coin money. But can a power
to impart these qualities to notes, or promises to pay
money, when offered in discharge of pre-existing debts,

be derived from the coinage power, or from any other
power expressly given? It is certainly not the same power
as the power to coin money.

Or, more succinctly: "The fundamental question, that which tests
the validity of the legislation, is, can Congress constitutionally
give to treasury notes the character and qualities of money?"

On the basis of the principle that "the power to levy and
collect taxes, to coin money and regulate its value . . . are instruments for the paramount object, which was to establish a government, sovereign within its sphere, with capability of self-
preservation," Justice Strong appealed to recent experience in the
Civil War: "Something revived the drooping faith of the people;
something brought immediately to the government's aid the resources of the nation, and something enabled the successful pros-
ecution of the war, and the preservation of the national life. What
was it, if not the legal tender enactments?" Indeed, "there are
some considerations touching these clauses which tend to show
that if any implications are to be deduced from them, they are of
an enlarging rather than a restraining character." Or, to put the
word "enlarging" in Newman's terms, paper money was therefore
to be regarded as a "preservative addition" to the coinage clause,
one whose "action upon its past" was "conservative."

"Seventh Note. Its Chronic Vigor [Chronic Continuance]"

The seventh and last of Newman's "tests" or "notes" of development was *chronic vigor*. It was in some ways a summary recapitulation of the other six. Because, he argued, "corruption cannot be of long standing," it followed that "*duration* is another
test of a faithful development." Like several of his other tests, this

one was applicable well beyond the dogmatic and ecclesiastical realm; for "sober men are indisposed to change in civil matters, and fear reforms and innovations, lest, if they go a little too far, they should at once run to some great calamities before a remedy can be applied." Newman the historian of doctrine concluded that, by contrast with the "continuance" and "vigor" of Catholic Christianity, "the course of heresies is always short." This note, therefore, could be said to consist "in its union of vigor with continuance, that is, in its tenacity."

A manifestation of this note of development of doctrine in the interpretation of Christian Scripture has been the *chronic vigor* of the insistence that the personal wickedness of a priest or bishop does not invalidate his ministry or sacraments. According to the New Testament, "Christ loved the church and gave himself up for her, that he might *sanctify* her . . . that she might be *holy and without blemish*" (Eph 5.25–27). The title "holy" was one of the earliest and most widely distributed attributes of the church in the creeds: "And I believe in the Holy Spirit, the holy church," a second-century symbol affirmed. In *The Niceno-Constantinopolitan Creed,* the title became the second in the classic affirmation of the four marks and attributes of the church: "one, holy, catholic, and apostolic." But by that time the ongoing experience of the early centuries had repeatedly demonstrated that neither the members nor the priests nor the bishops of the church were always moral or holy, and under the persecutions of the third and fourth centuries there had been unfaithful disciples in each of these classes. What did such unfaithfulness on the part of a bishop or a priest imply for the sacraments that believers had unwittingly received at his hands? The Catholic answer, as formulated above all by Augustine, was that the holiness of the church was to be defined sacramentally, not statistically: the command and promise of Christ for the sacraments and for ordination validated even the sacraments administered by an unworthy priest or bishop. Because the polemics of the Protestant Reformation against the Roman Catholic Church inevitably raised the question again, Augustine's answer demonstrated its durability and *chronic continuance* in the Reformation confessions, as well as in the responses to them. But also after the Reformation, the *chronic continuance* of the Augustinian answer maintained itself— as did, unfortunately, that of the saying of Jesus in the Gospel (Mt 26.41): "The spirit indeed is willing, but the flesh is weak." Even as seventeenth-century Congregationalists were radically subordinating the power of the sacraments to the primacy of the preaching of the word by insisting that "the grace which is exhibited in or by the sacraments rightly used, is not conferred by any power in them," they added: "neither doth the efficacy of a sacrament depend upon the piety or intention of him that doth administer it."

For the development of the interpretation of American Scripture, too, a summary recapitulation of the other notes can be found "in its union of vigor with continuance, that is, in its tenacity": the note and test with which American Scripture (as well as this examination of it) opened, "we the people." The *continuance* has been *chronic* through the expansion of thirteen colonies to fifty states, the industrialization and postindustrialization of an agricultural economy, the immigration of population from most of the nations of the globe, the belated but decisive extension to all citizens of the rights originally reserved for some, the scientific and technological transformation of an entire society, the burgeoning of religious pluralism. The content of "we the people" has shifted, the authority of "we the people" has continued and grown. Although the triumphalism may seem excessive to some present-day sensibilities, whether theological or political, the periodic sentences with which Newman opens his peroration on development in the *Essay on Development* can therefore, with relatively slight adaptation (indicated by square brackets), be applied to the *chronic vigor* of the constitutional system of "we the people":

> When we consider the succession of ages during which the [constitutional] system has endured, the severity of the trials it has undergone, the sudden and wonderful changes without and within which have befallen it, the incessant mental activity and the intellectual gifts of its maintainers, the enthusiasm which it has kindled, the fury of the controversies which have been carried on among its professors, the impetuosity of the assaults made upon it, the ever-increasing responsibilities to which it has been committed by the continuous development of its dogmas, it is quite inconceivable that it should not have been broken up and lost, were it a corruption [. . . .] Yet it is still living, if there be a living [. . .] philosophy in the world; vigorous, energetic, persuasive, progressive; *vires acquirit eundo* [it gathers strength as it moves along]; it grows and is not overgrown; it spreads out, yet is not enfeebled; it is ever germinating, yet ever consistent with itself.

Notes

1 Normative Scripture—Christian and American

2   "creeds, confessions, and biblical exegesis": See the Bibliography, in which I have included my principal works dealing with creeds and with the history of biblical interpretation.

2   "dissertation": Pelikan 1946; *First Bohemian Confession,* 1 Creeds 796–833 (1535).

2   " 'I have changed in many things' ": Newman [1864] 1967, 54.

2   " 'The Reformation superseded' ": Corwin 1959, 1.

3   "two chapters of *Credo*": *Credo,* 142–57, 273–77.

3   " 'confessional subscription' ": *Credo,* 264–73.

5   "normative Great Code": Frye 1982.

5   " 'not spake but speaketh!' ": Emerson [1838] 1992, 80.

6   " 'a house divided against itself' ": 6 *Schleitheim Confession,* 2 Creeds 701 (1527).

6   " 'ordinary language' of Americans": Brigham 1978, 98.

6   "seventeenth-century confession": 1.8; 1.11 *Canons of the Synod of Dort,* 2 Creeds 572–73 (1618–19).

6   " 'If regulation goes too far' ": Justice Oliver Wendell Holmes, Jr., for the Court, *Pennsylvania Coal Co.* v. *Mahon,* 260 U.S. 415 (1922).

6   " 'takings' ": Epstein 1985; Amar 1998, 77–80.

7   " 'eminent domain' ": *OED* 3:592.

7   "a massive lexicon of the Constitution": Greene 1991; Blaustein 1992.

7   " 'love and *reverence*' ": 21 *Decree on Ecumenism of the Second Vatican Council,* 3 Creeds 648 (1964); italics added.

7   *"Dogmatic Constitution": Dogmatic Constitution on Divine Revelation of the Second Vatican Council,* 3 Creeds 650–62 (1965).

7   "secular liturgy": Lerner 1937.

7   " 'The sessions of this court' ": *Abington School District* v. *Schempp,* 374 U.S. 213 (1963).

7   " 'A fastidious atheist' ": Justice William O. Douglas, for the Court, *Zorach* v. *Clauson,* 343 U.S. 313 (1952). See, in general, Shiffrin 1983.

7   "reduction in the private authority": As described in Carter 1987.

8   "substitute for the mystical experience": Barzun 1974.

8   " 'America would have no national church' ": Grey 1984, 18.

8   "that was to become axiomatic": For example, Justice Samuel Freeman Miller, dissenting, *Hepburn* v. *Griswold,* 75 U.S. 630 (1870).

8   " 'intended to endure for ages' ": Chief Justice John Marshall, for the Court, *McCulloch* v. *Maryland,* 17 U.S. 415 (1819); italics original.

8   "source and norm": 2 *A Brief Statement of the Doctrinal Position of the Evangelical Lutheran Synod of Missouri, Ohio, and Other States,* 3 Creeds 488 (1932).

8   " 'could not have been foreseen completely' ": Justice Oliver Wendell Holmes, Jr., for the Court, *Missouri* v. *Holland,* 252 U.S. 433 (1920).

9   " 'Time works changes' ": Justice Joseph McKenna, for the Court, *Weems* v. *United States,* 217 U.S. 373 (1910).

9   " 'in accordance with the Scriptures' ": 5 *Niceno-Constantinopolitan Creed,* 1 Creeds 163 (381).

10   " 'there are . . . parallels' ": Burt 1984, 467.

10   " 'language of the Constitution' ": *Ableman* v. *Booth* and *United States* v. *Booth,* 62 U.S. 517 (1859).

10   " 'The Constitution of the United States' ": Justice David Davis, for the Court, *Ex parte Milligan,* 71 U.S. 120–21 (1866).

10   *"The Belgic Confession":* 7 *Belgic Confession,* 2 Creeds 408–9 (1561); also preface *French Confession,* 2 Creeds 373 (1559/1571).

10   " 'Take note of those' ": 9.13 *First Bohemian Confession,* 1 Creeds
      816 (1535).

11   " 'it is not left in the power' ": 1.3 *Cambridge Platform,* 3 Creeds
      65 (1648).

11   " 'To maintain that our federal' ": Justice Samuel Chase, for the
      Court, *Calder* v. *Bull,* 3 U.S. 388–89 (1798); italics added.

11   " 'No *doctrine*' ": Justice David Davis, for the Court, *Ex parte
      Milligan,* 71 U.S. 121 (1866); italics added.

11   " 'tortured construction' ": Justice Harlan Fiske Stone, dissenting,
      United States v. *Butler,* 297 U.S. 87 (1936); 8 *Reckoning of the
      Faith,* 2 Creeds 264–65 (1530).

11   " 'strict and literal' interpretation": *McCulloch* v. *Maryland,* 17
      U.S. 354 (1819); 22 *Zurich Consensus,* 2 Creeds 811 (1549).

11   " 'strained, confused, and obscure subtleties' ": 11.9 *Second Hel-
      vetic Confession,* 2 Creeds 477 (1566).

11   " 'narrow and artificial' ": Justice John Marshall Harlan, dissent-
      ing, *Civil Rights Cases,* 109 U.S. 26 (1883); for the context of this
      in his thought, see Clark 1915.

11   " 'elusive at best' ": Justice Harry Andrew Blackmun, for the
      Court, *Garcia* v. *San Antonio Metropolitan Transit Authority,* 469
      U.S. 539 (1985).

11   "translation . . . involves interpretation": See pp. 108–14 below.

11   "legal hermeneutics": Vetter and Potacs 1990.

12   " 'Principles of Interpretation and Construction' ": Lieber 1880.

12   " 'the construction of the Constitution' ": Chief Justice Roger
      Brooke Taney for the Court, *Charles River Bridge* v. *Warren
      Bridge,* 36 U.S. 553 (1837); also Justice Peter Vivian Daniel, dis-
      senting, *The Propeller Genesee Chief* v. *Fitzhugh et al.,* 53 U.S. 464–
      65 (1852).

12   "the authentic canon": *Credo,* 139–41.

12   " 'the books commonly called Apocrypha' ": 1.3 *Westminster Con-
      fession,* 2 Creeds 606 (1647).

13   " 'written list of the sacred books' ": 4.1 *Decrees of the Council of
      Trent,* 2 Creeds 822–23 (1546).

13   "Greek Septuagint": See pp. 112–14 below.

13   "canon of the Constitution": I am indebted for this insight to
      Professor Bernard Bailyn.

13   "possibility of amending the Constitution": Dellinger 1983.

13   " 'preservative additions' ": Newman [1878] 1989, 303; see pp. 143–46 below.

13   "some similarities": Hand 1958.

14   "recent confessional statements repudiate": 16 *Dogmatic Constitution on the Church of the Second Vatican Council,* 3 Creeds 586–87 (1964).

14   " 'Christian Scripture' ": See pp. 112–14 below.

15   " 'the rule of prayer is the rule of faith' ": *Credo,* 166–78.

15   " 'religious ceremony' ": *Abington School District* v. *Schempp,* 374 U.S. 210; 223 (1963).

15   " 'invokes the grace of God' ": *Abington School District* v. *Schempp,* 374 U.S. 213 (1963).

15   " 'people of the Book' ": For example, Surah 5.77, where the primary reference is to Christianity, but in relation to Judaism.

15   "special relation": Lintott 1999; also Rahe 1992.

16   " 'law of Christ' ": 5 *Dordrecht Confession,* 2 Creeds 777 (1632); see *Christian Tradition,* 1:17–18, 38–39.

16   " 'sundry judicial laws' ": 19.3–4 *Westminster Confession,* 2 Creeds 629 (1647).

16   " 'nor the civil precepts thereof' ": 7 *Thirty-Nine Articles,* 2 Creeds 530 (1571); 84 *Irish Articles,* 2 Creeds 565 (1615).

17   "obeying the injunctions of Torah": King 1995.

17   " 'Shari'a *as* Constitution' ": Anderson 1959.

17   "a system for regulating personal conduct": Cook 2000.

17   "punishments prescribed by the Qur'an": Edge 1996.

17   " 'the criminal and civic laws of Islam' ": Chaudrhy 1997.

18   "Egyptian 'Law 44' ": Joheir 1983; Ascha 1997; al-Hibri 2001.

18   "evolution . . . of secular law in Turkey": Vergin 2001.

19   " 'the conception of political equality' ": Justice William O. Douglas, for the Court, *Gray* v. *Sanders,* 372 U.S. 381 (1963).

19   " 'the permanent rhetoric of the nation' ": Pollak 1966, 1:23.

20   "theistic basis for the doctrine of 'natural rights' ": Haines 1930; Wright 1931. See also Bradford 1993, 87–102.

20   "Constitutional Convention was 'scolded' ": Hutson 1998, 75–78.

20   " 'we are a religious people' ": Justice William O. Douglas, for the Court, *Zorach* v. *Clauson,* 343 U.S. 313 (1952).

20   "The Declaration . . . an authority": For example, Justice Smith
       Thompson, for the Court, *Inglis* v. *Trustees of Sailor's Snug Har-
       bour,* 28 U.S. 123, 125–26 (1830); Chief Justice Morrison Remick
       Waite, for the Court, *United States* v. *Cruikshank et al.,* 92 U.S.
       553 (1876).

20   "controversial opinion rendered by . . . Holmes": *Buck* v. *Bell,* 274
       U.S. 206–7 (1927); see pp. 135–36 below.

20   " 'he took the Constitution for his text' ": Menand 2001, 66.

21   " 'Constitution as a living document' ": T. Marshall 1987; italics
       original. See Ackerman 1991–98, 2:32–33.

21   " 'there are to-day no truer exponents' ": DuBois [1903] 1990, 14.

22   " 'Never has a sociopolitical document' ": Washington 1968, 219;
       119 (which also included a quotation from Frederick Douglass on
       the Constitution).

22   "logic of textual exegesis": Bernd 1968.

22   "*Brown* v. *Board of Education*": Patterson 2001.

22   " 'the power of an interpretive community' ": Fish 1980, 339; also
       Fiss 1982, 746; Brest 1982, 766–67.

22   " 'The constitution of the United States' ": Justice Joseph Story,
       Martin v. *Hunter's Lessee,* 14 U.S. 323 (1816).

23   " 'Do the People . . . form a Nation?' ": Justice James Wilson,
       Chisholm v. *Georgia,* 2 U.S. 453 (1793).

23   " 'This tribunal . . . was erected' ": *Ableman* v. *Booth* and *United
       States* v. *Booth,* 62 U.S. 521 (1859); italics added.

23   " 'a legal code' ": Chief Justice John Marshall, for the Court,
       McCulloch v. *Maryland,* 17 U.S. 407 (1819).

23   "a half-century later": Justice William Strong, for the Court, *Le-
       gal Tender Cases,* 79 U.S. 532 (1870).

23   " 'the Constitution is the fundamental law' ": Chief Justice Sal-
       mon Portland Chase, for the Court, *Hepburn* v. *Griswold,* 75 U.S.
       611 (1870).

23   " 'The censorial power' ": Justice William Joseph Brennan, Jr.,
       for the Court, *New York Times Co.* v. *Sullivan,* 376 U.S. 275
       (1964).

23   " 'ultimate protection' ": Frankfurter 1929, 235.

24   "the people have also retained": Barnet 1989–93.

24   " 'single, frightening' ": Gilmore 1977, 49.

24   " 'the first requirement of a sound body' ": Holmes 1881, 41; ital-
      ics added.

24   " 'When men have realized that time": Justice Oliver Wendell
      Holmes, Jr., dissenting, *Abrams* v. *United States*, 250 U.S. 630
      (1919). But see also Justice Oliver Wendell Holmes, Jr., dis-
      senting, *Lochner* v. *New York*, 198 U.S. 76 (1905), and p. 131 be-
      low.

24   "cumulative experience of 'we the people' ": Ackerman 1991–98.
      See also Sunstein 1987a, and White 2000.

25   " 'gives offense as being unknown' ": *Creed of the Fourth Synod of
      Sirmium*, 1 Creeds 98 (359).

25   " 'Those who, in the absence of written documents' ": *Rule of
      Faith of Irenaeus*, 1 Creeds 50 (c. 180).

25   " 'the entire church is unanimous' ": Origen 1.4–8 *On First Prin-
      ciples*, 1 Creeds 64–65 (c. 222–30).

25   "believing 'wise citizens' ": 6 *Edict of Michael Cerularius and the
      Synod of Constantinople*, 1 Creeds 314 (1054).

26   " 'neither patriarchs nor councils' ": 17 *Response of Eastern Ortho-
      dox Patriarchs to Pope Pius IX*, 3 Creeds 282 (1848); italics added.

26   " 'it is not necessary' ": 7–8 *Declaration and Address of Thomas
      Campbell*, 3 Creeds 221 (1809).

26   " 'interpret them to the people' ": 10.4 *First Bohemian Confession*,
      1 Creeds 817 (1535).

26   "*consensus fidelium*": Norris 1978.

27   "*magnus consensus*": 1; 7 *Augsburg Confession*, 2 Creeds 58; 62
      (1530).

27   " 'the protector of religion' ": 17 *Response of Eastern Orthodox Pa-
      triarchs to Pope Pius IX,* 3 Creeds 282 (1848); italics added.

27   " 'On Consulting the Faithful in Matters of Doctrine' ": Newman
      [1858] 1962.

27   "*Syllabus of Errors* . . . and . . . infallibility of the pope": 3 Creeds
      324–34 (1864); 3 Creeds 341–58 (1869–70).

27   " 'the universal consent of the fathers' ": 14.1 *Decrees of the Council
      of Trent*, 2 Creeds 849 (1551).

27   " 'The real significance of constitutional theory' ": Richard A.
      Posner in Dorsen 2002, 219.

28   " 'the chasm . . . between the world' ": Rabban 1981, 579.

28   " 'should not be employed in sermons' ": 1.13 *Formula of Concord: Epitome,* 2 Creeds 172 (1577).

28   " 'those things which are necessary' ": 1.7 *Westminster Confession,* 2 Creeds 607 (1647); italics added.

28   " 'caused our bishops . . . and *best learned men of our clergy* ' ": Preface to *The Ten Articles,* 2 Creeds 298 (1536); italics added.

28   "overemphasized learning": 1 *Confession of Hans Denck Before the Nuremberg Council,* 2 Creeds 668 (1525).

28   " 'innocent *and unlearned* persons' ": Preface to *Dordrecht Confession,* 2 Creeds 769 (1632); italics added.

29   " *'giving attendance to study and learning'* ": 34 *A True Confession of English Separatists,* 3 Creeds 42 (1596); italics added.

29   " 'excellent, great, or learned' ": 25 *A True Confession of English Separatists,* 3 Creeds 40 (1596); also 43 *First London Confession,* 3 Creeds 60 (1644).

29   " *'scientific [wissenschaftlich] method'* ": 9 *Fourteen Theses of the First [Old Catholic, Eastern Orthodox, and Anglican] Reunion Conference at Bonn,* 3 Creeds 367 (1874); italics added.

29   " 'theological and historical research' ": 5 *Decree on Ecumenism of the Second Vatican Council,* 3 Creeds 640 (1964).

29   " 'the one, that which is contained' ": Elert 1962, 9–10.

30   "*ēthos . . . pathos . . . logos*": Pelikan 2001.

30   "*sensus literalis* remains primary": See pp. 76–114 below.

30   "the Great Code": As noted earlier, however, "code" can sometimes carry a disparaging connotation: Chief Justice John Marshall, for the Court, *McCulloch* v. *Maryland,* 17 U.S. 407 (1819); Frankfurter 1929, 235.

30   " 'codes and codas' ": Daube 1969, 74–101.

30   "shares with any other code": OED 2:582–83.

30   " 'the teaching authority' ": 6 *Tome of the Synod of Constantinople,* 1 Creeds 321 (1341).

30   " 'the cult of the courts' ": Brigham 1987.

31   "The English word 'hierarchy' ": OED 5-I:272.

31   " 'understand, *interpret,* and proclaim it' ": 7 *Canons of the Council of Ephesus,* 1 Creeds 167 (431); italics added.

31   "normative interpretation of American Scripture": See also pp. 70–75 below.

31   " 'The doctrine of the separation of powers' ": Justice Louis D.
Brandeis, dissenting, *Myers* v. *United States*, 272 U.S. 293 (1926).

31   "the title 'ecumenical' ": Huizing and Walf 1983.

32   " 'distribution of powers' ": Tierney 1998; also pp. 70–75 below.

32   " 'draw on our merely personal and private notions' ": Justice Felix Frankfurter, for the Court, *Rochin* v. *California*, 342 U.S. 170
(1952).

32   " 'judges recuse themselves' ": Justice Felix Frankfurter, *Public
Utilities Commission* v. *Pollak*, 343 U.S. 466–67 (1952).

32   "subordinated his own moral and philosophical position": Justice
William Paterson, *Calder* v. *Bull*, 3 U.S. 395, 387 (1798); see
pp. 89–90 below.

32   " 'the false doctrine' ": 2; 6 *Barmen Declaration*, 3 Creeds 507–8
(1934).

34   " 'intellectual history that takes serious ideas seriously' ": Himmelfarb 1987, 9.

34   " 'personify ideas in themselves' ": Butterfield 1931, 43.

34   " 'flamboyant both in his personality' ": Gilmore 1977, 84.

34   " 'Judges are human' ": Llewellyn 1960, 201.

35   " 'the interference of extra-ecclesial interests' ": 8 *Balamand Declaration on Uniatism, Method of Union of the Past, and the Present
Search for Full Communion: Ecclesiological Principles*, 3 Creeds 849
(1993).

35   "does not justify reducing the textual and doctrinal debates":
Jones 1966.

35   " 'acts of constitutional *interpretation*' ": Ackerman 1991–98, 1:132;
italics original.

35   "New Deal": See also White 2000.

35   "*Dred Scott* decision": Kutler 1967.

35   " 'At the very least, if doctrine did not determine' ": Pelikan
1990a, 39.

36   " 'textualists' ": Grey 1984, 1, where the contrast drawn is with
those whom he calls "supplementers."

36   "*The Theodosian Code*": Credo, 225–29.

36   "one of the most carefully wrought confessions": *Edict of Justinian*, 1 Creeds 122–49 (551).

36   "christological confession": 1.A.5 *Liturgy of Saint John Chrysostom,*
      1 Creeds 273.

36   "scholarship in the history of law": Kriele 1999.

36   "outstanding examples": Daube 1969; Berman 1993; Noonan
      1987.

36   "four-volume examination": Witte 2002.

37   "other recent books": For example, McConnell, Cochran, and
      Carmella 2001.

37   *"antidōrea":* Aristotle *Nicomachean Ethics* 1123a3.

2   Cruxes of Interpretation in the Bible and in the Constitution

38   " 'a difficulty which it torments' ": *OED* 2:1226.

39   " 'consubstantial, one in being' ": 2 *The Niceno-Constantinopolitan
      Creed,* 1 Creeds 163 (381).

39   "orthodox interpreters of all denominations": *Christian Tradition,*
      1:245–46; 2:59; 3:53; 5:101, 143.

39   " 'the embarrassing Second Amendment' ": Levinson 1989.

39   " 'obscure' ": See pp. 106–7 below.

39   " 'You are called upon to deliberate' ": *The Federalist* No. 1
      (Cooke 1961, 3).

40   " 'after an unequivocal experience' ": H. Black 1968, 6.

40   "superseded by the ratification": Beeman, Botein, and Carter 1987;
      Max Farrand in Hall 1987, 146–58.

41   "in their total practice": Pelikan 1992.

41   " 'the Quotations and Texts of Scripture Annexed' ": *Westminster
      Confession,* 2 Creeds 604 (1647).

41   " 'to read *and search them*' ": 1.8 *Westminster Confession,* 2 Creeds
      607 (1647); italics added.

41   "biblical proof texts": *Credo,* 136–38.

41   " 'if Divine Scripture were clear' ": 1.2 *Confession of Dositheus,* 1
      Creeds 632 (1672); italics added.

43   " 'would go in among his disciples' ": 11 *Tome of Leo,* 1 Creeds 118–
      19 (449).

43 " 'beginning with Moses' ": 1.54 *Confession of Peter Mogila,* 1
Creeds 585 (1638/1642).

43 "Christian pedagogy": Bousset 1915. See also pp. 104–8 below.

45 " 'the thickness of legal meaning' ": Cover 1983, 19–25.

45 " 'the impossibility of a clause-bound interpretivism' ": Ely 1980,
1–41.

45 " 'All who say that the gospel' ": 1 *Sixty-Seven Articles of Ulrich
Zwingli,* 2 Creeds 209 (1523).

46 " 'The interpretation of Scripture' ": 18 *Scots Confession,* 2 Creeds
398–99 (1560); italics added.

46 " 'We hold that interpretation of the Scriptures' ": 2.1 *Second Helvetic Confession,* 2 Creeds 462 (1566); numbers in brackets added.
See *Credo,* 142–60.

46 " 'it is impossible that I should entirely understand the Scripture' ": 1 *Confession of Hans Denck Before the Nuremberg Council,* 2
Creeds 668 (1525).

47 " 'the great Inspirer of Scripture' ": 4 *Richmond Declaration of
Faith of the Friends Yearly Meeting,* 3 Creeds 381–82 (1887).

47 " 'No one, relying on his personal judgment' ": 4.2 *Council of
Trent,* 2 Creeds 823 (1546).

47 " 'The Holy Scriptures were entrusted": 7.9 *Confession of Metrophanes Critopoulos,* 1 Creeds 513 (1625).

48 " 'has authority, in her general councils' ": 1.85 *Confession of Peter
Mogila,* 1 Creeds 597 (1638/1642).

48 " 'influence of Anglo-American' ": In Dorsen 2002, 211.

48 " 'attacks on the legitimacy' ": Powell 1985, 891.

48 "exposition of hermeneutical method": Moldaenke 1936; "Exegesis and Hermeneutics," Pelikan 1996, 22–39.

48 " 'Thereupon we ask, not what this man meant' ": Holmes 1899,
417–19.

49 " 'The influence of constitution worship' ": Levi 1949, 59–61.

49 " 'interpretations' in the plural": Krausz 2002.

49 " 'freewheeling' ": Epstein 1992, 701–2; Henry and LeFrancois
2002, 258.

49 " 'Humpty-Dumpty textual manipulation' ": C. Black 1969, 29.

49 " 'textual support in the constitutional language' ": Justice Byron

Raymond White, for the Court, *Bowers* v. *Hardwick,* 478 U.S. 191 (1986).

50   " 'a constructivist coherence theory' ": Fallon 1987, 1189–90.

50   " 'interpretation was a hot topic' ": Posner 1998, 209.

50   " 'The question of interpretation now enjoys' ": Epstein 1992, 699.

50   " 'interpretivism had a bad reputation' ": Tushnet 1983, 787.

50   " 'It comes down to two propositions' ": Posner 1998, 209–11.

51   "In interpreting a law": Justice David Davis, for the Court, *Ex parte Milligan,* 71 U.S. 114 (1866).

51   " 'what the statute *means*' ": Holmes 1899, 417–19.

51   "rules of confessional hermeneutics": *Credo,* 273–77.

51   " 'the quiet instants' ": Henry James *The Ambassadors* ch. 7.

51   "Berengar of Tours": *First Confession of Berengar; Second Confession of Berengar,* 1 Creeds 728–29 (1059; 1079).

51   "most important dogmatic difference": 15 *Marburg Articles,* 2 Creeds 795 (1529).

51   "chapter titles and historical periodizations": *Christian Tradition,* 3:74–80, 204–14; 4:158–61, 189–203.

52   *"lectio divina":* Leclercq 1982, 76–93.

52   "central component of lay piety": For example 77; 39 *Confession of Faith of the Cumberland Presbyterian Church,* 3 Creeds 236; 230 (1814/1883); 26 *Confessional Statement of the United Presbyterian Church of North America,* 3 Creeds 463 (1925).

52   " 'by the testimony and inward illumination' ": 4 *French Confession,* 2 Creeds 376 (1559/71).

53   " 'remains a classic' ": *ODCC* 188; Pelikan 1952.

53   " 'according to the internal order' ": Chenu 1964, 220, 250.

53   *"Marbury* v. *Madison":* Chief Justice John Marshall, for the Court, *Marbury* v. *Madison,* 5 U.S. 168 (1803).

54   " 'An essay on Blackstone's Commentaries' ": Boorstin [1941] 1996.

54   " 'consistent with the constitution and laws' ": Justice Joseph Story, for the Court, *Martin* v. *Hunter's Lessee* 14 U.S. 361 (1816); see Newmeyer 1985.

54   *"Commentaries on the Constitution":* Story [1883] 1994.

54   " 'anxiously and deliberately' ": *Ableman* v. *Booth* and *United States* v. *Booth*, 62 U.S. 522 (1859).

55   "his strongly voiced opinions": Yarbrough 1988; Freyer 1990.

55   " 'That Constitution is my legal bible' ": H. Black 1968, 64, 66.

55   " 'No doctrine is defined' ": Newman [1878] 1989, 151.

55   "*magisterium* of the church": Congar 1976.

55   "conciliar and confessional usage": "Sequentes divinitus inspira-tum sanctorum patrum nostrorum *magisterium* et catholicae trad-itionem ecclesiae": *Decree of the Second Council of Nicaea* (Latin version), 1 Creeds 236 (787).

56   " 'what the church of Jesus Christ believes' ": *Christian Tradition*, 1:1.

56   " 'by divine and Catholic faith' ": 3 *Dogmatic Constitution of the First Vatican Council on the Catholic Faith*, 3 Creeds 347 (1870).

56   " 'The doctrine of the Double Procession' ": Quoted from the Sermon on Development of 1843 by Chadwick 1957, 235.

57   " 'Neither patriarchs nor councils' ": 17 *Response of the Eastern Pa-triarchs to Pope Pius IX*, 3 Creeds 282 (1848); see p. 26 above.

57   " 'written and unwritten tradition' ": *Decree of the Second Council of Nicaea*, 1 Creeds 237; 241 (787).

57   " 'the emancipation of exegesis' ": *Lamentabili of Pope Pius X*, 3 Creeds 403 (1907).

58   " 'The court are fully sensible' ": Chief Justice Roger Brooke Ta-ney, for the Court, *Charles River Bridge* v. *Warren Bridge*, 36 U.S. 535; 553 (1837).

58   " 'a perpetual censor' ": Justice Samuel Freeman Miller, for the Court, *Slaughterhouse Cases*, 83 U.S. 78 (1873).

58   " 'without authority to pass *abstract opinions*' ": Justice George Sutherland, for the Court, *Massachusetts* v. *Mellon*, 262 U.S. 485 (1923); italics added.

58   " 'Congress must obey the Constitution' ": Justice Potter Stewart, dissenting, *Fullilove* v. *Klutznick*, 448 U.S. 526–27 (1980).

58   " 'we refrain from passing upon the constitutionality' ": Justice Mahlon Pitney, for the Court, *Blair* v. *United States*, 250 U.S. 279 (1919).

59   " 'a series of rules' ": Justice Louis Dembits Brandeis, *Ashwander* v. *Valley Authority*, 297 U.S. 346–48 (1936).

59   " 'is legitimate only in the last resort' ": *Chicago & Grand Trunk Railway* v. *Wellman,* 143 U.S. 345 (1892).

59   " 'anticipate a question of constitutional law' ": Justice Thomas Stanley Matthews, for the Court, *Liverpool, N. Y. & P. S. Co.* v. *Emigration Commissioners,* 113 U.S. 39 (1885).

59   " 'formulate a rule of constitutional law' ": *Liverpool, N. Y. & P. S. Co.* v. *Emigration Commissioners,* 113 U.S. 39 (1885).

59   " 'When the validity of an act of Congress' ": Chief Justice Charles Evans Hughes, for the Court, *Crowell* v. *Benson,* 285 U.S. 62 (1932).

60   " 'there may be narrower scope' ": Justice Harlan Fiske Stone, for the Court, *United States* v. *Carolene Products Co.,* 304 U.S. 152n (1938).

60   " 'brooding omnipresence' ": Justice John Marshall Harlan, dissenting, *Katzenbach* v. *Morgan,* 384 U.S. 670 (1966); see Curtis 1986.

60   " 'no set of legal institutions or prescriptions' ": Cover 1983, 4.

60   " 'literary genres' ": 12 *Dogmatic Constitution of the Second Vatican Council on Divine Revelation,* 3 Creeds 656 (1965).

60   "similarities noted by Robert Burt": Burt 1984.

61   " 'especially constitutes the word of God' ": 6 *Statement of Belief of the Seventh-Day Adventist Church,* 3 Creeds 361 (1872).

61   "makes an article on the Last Judgment necessary": 7 *Niceno-Constantinopolitan Creed,* 1 Creeds 163 (381); 17 *Augsburg Confession,* 2 Creeds 68 (1530); 33 *Westminster Confession,* 2 Creeds 646–47 (1647).

61   "erotic imagery of the Song of Songs": Matter 1990.

61   "confusing array of ambiguities": Harris 1993, 114–63.

61   " 'Words being symbols' ": Justice Felix Frankfurter, for the Court, *Rochin* v. *California,* 342 U.S. 169 (1952).

61   " 'It is no very uncommon paradox' ": Tierney 1964, 72.

61   " 'explaining and reconciling apparently contradictory passages' ": 11.10 *Second Helvetic Confession,* 2 Creeds 477 (1566).

62   "harmonize with one another": 2.5 *Second Helvetic Confession,* 2 Creeds 462 (1566).

62   " 'an atmosphere of unconstitutionality' ": Justice Felix Frankfurter, concurring, *Korematsu* v. *United States,* 323 U.S. 224–25 (1944).

62 " 'running . . . into each other' ": Justice Tom Clark, for the
    Court, *Mapp* v. *Ohio*, 367 U.S. 646 (1961), quoting *Boyd* v.
    United States, 116 U.S. 630 (1886).

62 "proof of a plurality": Pelikan 1990b.

62 " 'union of nature indivisible' ": 28 *Tome of the Synod of Constanti-
    nople*, 1 Creeds 353 (1351).

63 " 'James does not contradict' ": 15.6 *Second Helvetic Confession*, 2
    Creeds 488 (1566).

63 " 'by that faith alone' ": 6.16 *Decrees of the Council of Trent*, 2
    Creeds 835–37 (1547).

63 "Eastern Orthodox confession": 1.1 *Confession of Peter Mogila*, 1
    Creeds 562 (1638/1642).

63 "An important constitutional illustration": Kalven 1964.

64 " 'preferred position' ": Justice William O. Douglas, for the
    Court, *Murdock* v. *Pennsylvania*, 319 U.S. 115 (1943).

64 "Jehovah's Witnesses": Chief Justice Charles Evans Hughes, for
    the Court, *Lovell* v. *City of Griffin*, 303 U.S. 450–52 (1938).

64 " 'functions to protect religion' ": Levy 1999, 102.

64 " 'irreconcilable conflict with the Free Exercise Clause' ": Justice
    Potter Stewart, dissenting, *Abington School District* v. *Schempp*, 374
    U.S. 309 (1963).

64 " 'these two clauses . . . overlap' ": Justice Tom Clark, for the
    Court, *Abington School District v. Schemp*, 374 U.S. 221 (1963), cit-
    ing previous opinions of the Court.

65 "both intended to forbid": Gillette 1969.

65 " 'unnecessary to consider the Fifteenth Amendment' ": Justice
    Oliver Wendell Holmes, Jr., for the Court, *Nixon* v. *Herndon*, 273
    U.S. 540–41 (1927).

65 " 'the well-established principle' ": Justice Stanley Forman Reed,
    for the Court, *Smith* v. *Allwright*, 321 U.S. 666 (1944).

65 " 'special discriminatory treatment' ": Justice Felix Frankfurter, for
    the Court, *Gomillion* v. *Lightfoot*, 364 U.S. 346 (1960).

65 " 'decision should be rested": Justice Charles Evans Whittaker,
    concurring, *Gomillion* v. *Lightfoot*, 364 U.S. 349 (1960).

65 "Justice Owen Roberts": Justice Owen Roberts, for the Court,
    Hague, Mayor, et al. v. *Congress of Industrial Organizations*, 307
    U.S. 512 (1939).

65   "Justice Harlan Fiske Stone": Justice Harlan Fiske Stone, concurring, *Hague, Mayor, et al.* v. *Congress of Industrial Organizations,* 307 U.S. 519 (1939).

65   "Pauline epistles": See pp. 76–79 below.

66   "great exegetical masters": DeLubac 1998–2000.

66   " 'his vain *allegories*' ": *King's Confession,* 2 Creeds 543 (1581); italics added.

66   " 'said to *be* that which they *signify*' ": 22 *Zurich Consensus,* 2 Creeds 811 (1549); italics added.

66   " 'a clash of absolutes' ": Tribe 1992.

67   "an almost statistical criterion": Berkson 1975.

67   " 'whether to the average person' ": Justice William Joseph Brennan, Jr., for the Court, *Roth* v. *United States,* 354 U.S. 489 (1957).

67   " 'it is neither realistic not constitutionally sound' ": Chief Justice Warren Earl Burger, for the Court, *Miller* v. *California,* 413 U.S. 20, 32 (1973).

67   " 'vague tests' ": Justice William O. Douglas, dissenting, *Miller* v. *California,* 413 U.S. 39 (1973).

67   " 'eternal verities' ": Chief Justice Warren Earl Burger, for the Court, *Miller* v. *California,* 413 U.S. 23 (1973).

67   " 'contemporary community standards' ": Schauer 1979; Ball and Pocock 1988.

67   " 'condemned by the light of nature' ": 14.3 *Cambridge Platform,* 3 Creeds 84 (1648).

68   " '*according to the standards*' ": 13 *Preface to Luther's Small Catechism,* 2 Creeds 32 (1529); italics added.

68   "in some Protestant confessions": 22 *Scots Confession,* 2 Creeds 402 (1560); 20.6 *Second Helvetic Confession,* 2 Creeds 510 (1566).

68   "permitting baptism by a woman": 3 *Doctrinal Decree of the Fourth Lateran Council,* 1 Creeds 742 (1215).

68   " 'some hard things in the Scriptures' ": 84; 5 *Irish Articles,* 2 Creeds 565; 554 (1615).

69   " 'circumstances in which' ": 2.1 *Second Helvetic Confession,* 2 Creeds 462 (1566).

69   " 'a Christian . . . acteth differently' ": 14.2 *Westminster Confession,* 2 Creeds 623 (1647); 14.2 *Savoy Declaration of Faith and Order,* 3 Creeds 117 (1658).

69 " 'contemporary community standards' ": Justice William Joseph Brennan, Jr., for the Court, *Roth* v. *United States,* 354 U.S. 489 (1957).

69 " 'general principles of law' ": Justice Samuel Chase, *Calder* v. *Bull,* 3 U.S. 388–89 (1798).

69 "concept of natural law": Haines 1930; Wright 1931; above all, Corwin 1959.

69 " 'eternal, objective, and universal law' ": 3 *Declaration on Religious Freedom of the Second Vatican Council,* 3 Creeds 664 (1965).

69 "is it knowable": Vögele 2000.

69 " 'principles of natural justice' ": *Charles River Bridge* v. *Warren Bridge,* 36 U.S. 452–53 (1837).

69 " 'general principles of law' ": Justice Samuel Chase, *Calder* v. *Bull,* 3 U.S. 388 (1798).

70 " 'condemned by the light of nature' ": 14.3 *Cambridge Platform,* 3 Creeds 84 (1648); also 10 *Faith and Practice of Thirty Congregations Gathered According to the Primitive Pattern,* 3 Creeds 94 (1651).

70 "a civil offense, not only a sin": 24.3 *Savoy Declaration of Faith and Order,* 3 Creeds 125 (1658); also 17.8 *Cambridge Platform,* 3 Creeds 91 (1648).

70 "stretched to include": Levy 1993.

70 "principles of the moral order": 14 *Declaration on Religious Freedom of the Second Vatican Council,* 3 Creeds 672 (1965).

70 " 'supreme law of society' ": 11 *Social Creed of Methodism,* 3 Creeds 416 (1908).

70 " '*Christian* principles of justice' ": 38 *Confessional Statement of the United Presbyterian Church,* 3 Creeds 468 (1925); italics added.

71 " 'other orthodox councils' ": 1.72 *Confession of Mogila,* 2 Creeds 593 (1638/1642).

71 " 'Even though the grace of the Holy Spirit' ": *Second Council of Constantinople,* 1 Creeds 185–87 (553).

72 " 'an ecumenical council' ": 15 *Response of the Eastern Patriarchs to Pope Pius IX,* 3 Creeds 279 (1848).

72 "defenders of papal authority": 3 *First Dogmatic Constitution of the First Vatican Council on the Church of Christ,* 3 Creeds 356 (1870).

72 " 'primacy of jurisdiction' ": 1 *First Dogmatic Constitution of the First Vatican Council on the Church of Christ,* 3 Creeds 353 (1870).

72 " 'whoever succeeds to the chair of Peter' ": 2 *First Dogmatic Constitution of the First Vatican Council on the Church of Christ,* 3 Creeds 354 (1870).

72 " 'preeminence of ordinary power' ": 3 *First Dogmatic Constitution of the First Vatican Council on the Church of Christ,* 3 Creeds 355 (1870).

72 " 'as a divinely revealed dogma' ": 4 *First Dogmatic Constitution of the First Vatican Council on the Church of Christ,* 3 Creeds 358 (1870).

73 "the apostles": 1 *Brief Statement,* 3 Creeds 488 (1932).

73 "their legitimate successors": *Second Council of Constantinople,* 1 Creeds 185–87 (553).

73 " 'the ordinary means' ": 1.7 *Westminster Confession,* 2 Creeds 607 (1647); italics added.

73 " 'directly, without means' ": 39 *Confession of the Cumberland Presbyterian Church,* 3 Creeds 230 (1814/1883).

73 " 'the federal judiciary is supreme' ": Chief Justice Earl Warren, for the Court, *Cooper* v. *Aaron,* 358 U.S. 18 (1958).

73 " 'as ultimate interpreter of the Constitution' ": Justice William Joseph Brennan, Jr., for the Court, *Baker* v. *Carr,* 369 U.S. 211 (1962).

73 " 'it is a singular fact' ": Thayer 1893, 129.

74 " 'notable case' ": Chief Justice Earl Warren, for the Court, *Cooper* v. *Aaron,* 358 U.S. 18 (1958).

74 "*Marbury* v. *Madison*": See the discussion in Clinton 1989, especially 81–101.

74 " '*the particular phraseology*' ": Chief Justice John Marshall, for the Court, *Marbury* v. *Madison,* 5 U.S. 180 (1803); italics added.

74 " 'logical sequence' ": Newman [1878] 1989, 189–95, 383–99; see pp. 137–40 below.

74 "The content of *Marbury*": *Federalist* No. 78 (1788) (Cooke 1961, 521–30) (Alexander Hamilton); see pp. 90–91 below.

74 "scholarly controversy about 'judicial review' ": Choper 1980; Hall 1985; Slotnick 1987.

75   " 'all are obliged to abide' ": *Dogmatic Constitution of the Second Vatican Council on the Church,* 3 Creeds 598 (1964); italics added.

3   The *Sensus Literalis* and the Quest for Original Intent

76   " 'could not have been foreseen' ": Justice Oliver Wendell Holmes, Jr., for the Court, *Missouri v. Holland,* 252 U.S. 433 (1920).

77   " 'a knowledge according to the letter' ": 20.5 *Mennonite Articles of Faith,* 3 Creeds 173 (1766/1895/1902).

77   " 'doctrine of the law' ": 13.4 *Second Helvetic Confession,* 2 Creeds 482 (1566); see also 10.3 *Bohemian Confession,* 1 Creeds 817 (1535).

77   " 'letter of the law' ": 6.1 *Decrees of the Council of Trent,* 2 Creeds 827 (1547).

77   " 'the infallible rule of interpretation' ": 1.9 *Westminster Confession,* 2 Creeds 608 (1647).

78   " 'everything required to satisfy' ": 1 *Luther's Small Catechism,* 2 Creeds 39 (1529).

78   " 'reason of the law is the soul' ": Quoted by Justice John Marshall Harlan, dissenting, *Civil Rights Cases,* 109 U.S. 26 (1883).

78   " *'the letter and spirit' "*: Chief Justice John Marshall, *McCulloch v. Maryland,* 17 U.S. 421 (1819); italics added.

79   " 'Then there is the doctrine' ": 1.8 Origen *On First Principles,* 1 Creeds 64–65 (c. 220–30).

79   " 'the Old Testament . . . represents' ": Daniélou 1960, 282.

79   " 'It may be almost laid down' ": Newman [1878] 1989, 344.

79   " 'fuller meaning' ": Brown 1955.

79   " 'strict textualism and intentionalism' ": Brest 1980, 223.

79   " *'deduced from scripture' "*: 1.6 *Savoy Declaration of Faith and Order,* 3 Creeds 107 (1658); italics added.

79   " 'analogical extensions' ": Epstein 1992, 713.

80   " 'speech will not be free' ": Pool 1983, 226.

80   "it is not indispensable": Justice William Strong, for the Court, *Legal Tender Cases,* 79 U.S. 534 (1870); italics added.

80   " 'some invisible radiation' ": Justice Oliver Wendell Holmes, Jr.,

for the Court, *Missouri* v. *Holland,* 252 U.S. 433–34 (1920). See also Lofgren 1980.

80   " 'nebulous standard' ": Justice Hugo L. Black, concurring, *Rochin* v. *California,* 342 U.S. 175 (1952).

81   " 'the First Amendment has a penumbra' ": Justice William O. Douglas, for the Court, *Griswold* v. *Connecticut,* 381 U.S. 484; 483 (1965).

81   " *'the Framers did not intend' "*: Justice Arthur J. Goldberg, *Griswold* v. *Connecticut,* 381 U.S. 494; 490 (1965); italics added.

81   " 'I get nowhere in this case' ": Justice Hugo L. Black, dissenting, *Griswold* v. *Connecticut,* 381 U.S. 508–10 (1965); italics added.

82   " 'We learn from the words of the Gospel' ": *Unam Sanctam,* 1 Creeds 746–47 (1302).

83   " 'right to depose emperors' ": 12 *Dictatus Papae of Gregory VII,* 1 Creeds 731 (c. 1075).

83   "this doctrine had developed": Ullmann 1949.

83   " 'by divine right possesses' ": 1–4 *Treatise on the Power and Primacy of the Pope,* 2 Creeds 150 (1537).

83   " 'improperly confused' ": 28.1 *Augsburg Confession,* 2 Creeds 104 (1530).

83   " 'doctrine of just war' ": 16.2 *Augsburg Confession,* 2 Creeds 67 (1530).

83   " 'against all use of force' ": 14 *Dordrecht Confession,* 2 Creeds 781 (1632); also already 6 *Schleitheim Confession,* 2 Creeds 699–701 (1527).

83   " 'sword into the hands of magistrates' ": 39 *French Confession,* 2 Creeds 385 (1559/1571). Traditionally, the "first table" embraced the commandments pertaining to duties toward God (whether three, by Roman Catholic and Lutheran counting, or four, by Eastern Orthodox and Reformed counting), the "second table" those (seven or six) pertaining to duties toward the neighbor: 19.2 *Savoy Declaration of Faith and Order,* 3 Creeds 120 (1658).

83   " 'at times in the life of the people' ": 11–12 *Declaration of the Second Vatican Council on Religious Freedom,* 3 Creeds 670–71 (1965).

84   " 'unwritten traditions": 4 *Anathemas of the Second Council of Nicaea Concerning Holy Images,* 1 Creeds 241 (787); 4.1 *Decrees of the Council of Trent,* 2 Creeds 822 (1546).

84   " 'making the express guarantees' ": *Griswold* v. *Connecticut*, 381 U.S. 484; 483 (1965).

84   " 'Christ's doctrine": Conclusion *Tetrapolitan Confession*, 2 Creeds 246–47 (1530); italics added.

84   " 'ground of our religion' ": 1 *Irish Articles*, 2 Creeds 552 (1615).

84   " 'textual support' ": Justice Byron Raymond White, for the Court, *Bowers* v. *Hardwick*, 478 U.S. 191 (1986); see Brigham 1978.

84   " 'arguments from the plain, necessary, or historical' ": Fallon 1987; see pp. 49–50 above.

85   " 'eyewitnesses from the beginning' ": 7 *Dogmatic Constitution on Divine Revelation of the Second Vatican Council*, 3 Creeds 653 (1965).

86   " 'apostolic' primacy": *Credo*, 104–7.

86   " 'without doubt the mother' ": 1.84 *Confession of Mogila*, 1 Creeds 596 (1638/42).

86   " *'in its original simplicity' "*: 1; 21 *Response of the Eastern Orthodox Patriarchs to Pope Pius IX*, 3 Creeds 266; 285 (1848); italics added.

86   " 'The supreme judge' ": 1.10 *Westminster Confession*, 2 Creeds 608 (1647).

87   " 'devised, imposed, stinted popish liturgy' ": 30 *True Confession of the English Separatists*, 3 Creeds 41 (1596).

87   " 'nearest to *the first institution*' ": 21.12 *Second Helvetic Confession*, 2 Creeds 514 (1566); italics added.

87   " *'custom of the primitive church' "*: 72 *Irish Articles*, 2 Creeds 564 (1615); italics added.

87   " 'gathered according to *the primitive pattern*' ": *The Faith and Practice of Thirty Congregations Gathered According to the Primitive Pattern*, 3 Creeds 92–100 (1651); italics added.

87   " 'same organization that existed": 6 *Articles of Faith of the Church of Jesus Christ of Latter-Day Saints*, 3 Creeds 257 (1842); italics added.

87   " *'primitive zeal' "*: George Eliot *Middlemarch* Book V, chapter 50; italics added.

88   "creedal and dogmatic tradition": *Credo*, 472–80.

88   "But later Protestants": 9 *Definite Platform*, 3 Creeds 314–15 (1855).

88   " 'distentangled from the accruing embarrassment' ": *Declaration and Address*, 3 Creeds 219 (1809); italics added.

88   "change of only one word": Bradford 1993.

88   " 'ceded to the General Government' ": *Ableman* v. *Booth* and *United States* v. *Booth*, 62 U.S. 517 (1859).

89   " 'intention of the great instrument' ": *Ableman* v. *Booth* and *United States* v. *Booth*, 62 U.S. 522 (1859).

89   "William Paterson": Levy 1999, 89.

89   " 'obviously the intention of the framers' ": Justice William Paterson, *Hylton* v. *United States*, 3 U.S. 176 (1796); italics added.

90   " 'It is obvious from the specification of contracts": Justice William Paterson, *Calder* v. *Bull*, 3 U.S. 395, 397 (1798); italics added.

90   " 'the particular phraseology' ": Chief Justice John Marshall, for the Court, *Marbury* v. *Madison*, 5 U.S. 180 (1803).

91   " 'There is no position' ": *Federalist* No. 78 (Cooke 1961, 524–25); italics original.

91   " 'unwritten traditions' ": 4.1 *Decrees of the Council of Trent*, 2 Creeds 822 (1546).

92   " 'whether the latter squares' ": Justice Owen Josephus Roberts, for the Court, *United States* v. *Butler*, 297 U.S. 62 (1936).

92   " 'Judges, who serve on good behavior' ": Epstein 1985, 19–20.

92   " 'in the same meaning' ": 1 *Wittenberg Articles*, 2 Creeds 15 (1536); italics added.

93   " 'We are to understand' ": Piepkorn 1993, 19–20.

93   " 'design or intention of the author' ": Wimsatt 1954, 3.

94   "as cited in the preceding chapter": See p. 50 above.

94   " 'Interpretation is not much' ": Posner 1998, 209–11.

94   "some critics have concluded": Abrams 1989.

94   " 'for the training up' ": 6.6; 4.4 *Cambridge Platform*, 3 Creeds 72; 69 (1648); see also 23.4 *Mennonite Articles of Faith*, 3 Creeds 177 (1766/1895/1902).

94   " 'superficial professors' ": 11 *New Hampshire Confession*, 3 Creeds 246 (1833/1853); also "mere professors," 11 *Baptist Faith and Message*, 3 Creeds 440 (1925).

95   "studying law and literature": Ward 1995; Ledwon 1996; Rockwood 1996.

95   "the enforceably normative": Levinson 1979, 123; Grey 1984, 3; Garet 1985, 111–12.

95   " 'judicial interpretation is authoritative' ": Fiss 1982, 755–56; Cover 1983, 43.

96   " 'character of the text' ": R. L. Marshall 1972, 1:218–29.

96   " 'the "authentic" performance' ": Kirkpatrick 1984, 126.

97   " 'the composer's advocate' ": Leinsdorf 1981, 170.

97   " 'If one had never heard' ": ap. Plaskin 1983, 221–22.

97   " 'of all Stravinsky's works' ": Vlad 1960, 92.

97   " '*Le Sacre* is arduous' ": Stravinsky and Craft 1981, 145.

98   "by later musicologists": van den Toorn 1983, 99–143.

98   "Justice Black's 'confessional' ": H. Black 1968, 64, 66; see p. 55 above.

98   " 'Time to taste life' ": Robert Browning "A Grammarian's Funeral," lines 55–61, 125–27.

99   " 'original intent relevant' ": Powell 1985, 887–88.

99   " 'An awareness of history' ": Justice William Joseph Brennan, Jr., *Abington School District* v. *Schempp,* 374 U.S. 234–41 (1963).

100   " 'Textual Support in the Constitutional Language' ": Justice Byron Raymond White, for the Court, *Bowers* v. *Hardwick,* 478 U.S. 191 (1986).

100   " 'proper relation to the times' ": 5 *Irish Articles,* 2 Creeds 554 (1615).

100   "medieval sacrament of penance": 17 *Council of Basel-Ferrara-Florence-Rome: Bull of Union with the Armenians,* 1 Creeds 761 (1439).

101   " 'fond thing vainly invented' ": 22 *Thirty-Nine Articles,* 2 Creeds 534 (1571); *OED* 4:395.

101   "biblical proof text for it": 50 *Dogmatic Constitution of the Second Vatican Council on the Church,* 3 Creeds 623 (1964); biblical translation as quoted there.

101   "yet doth [the church] not apply": 6 *Thirty-Nine Articles,* 2 Creeds 530 (1571).

102   " 'those ridiculous interpreters' ": 22 *Zurich Agreement,* 3 Creeds 811 (1549).

102   " 'approving and accepting the literal' ": 14.1 *Decrees of the Council of Trent,* 3 Creeds 849–50 (1551).

102 " 'textual support in the constitutional language' ": Justice Byron Raymond White, for the Court, *Bowers* v. *Hardwick,* 478 U.S. 191 (1986).

102 " 'borrow[ed] . . . our system of jurisprudence' ": Chief Justice Roger Brooke Taney, for the Court, *Charles River Bridge* v. *Warren Bridge,* 36 U.S. 545 (1837).

102 " 'performed, upon the sea' ": Justice Joseph Story, for the Court, *Thomas Jefferson,* 23 U.S. 429 (1825).

103 " 'navigable character of the water' ": Chief Justice Roger Brooke Taney, for the Court, *The Propeller Genesee Chief* v. *Fitzhugh et al.,* 53 U.S. 457 (1852).

103 " 'It is admitted that by the decisions in England' ": Justice Peter Vivian Daniel, dissenting, *The Propeller Genesee Chief* v. *Fitzhugh et al.,* 53 U.S. 464–65 (1852).

104 " 'come fairly and firmly' ": *Declaration and Address,* 3 Creeds 219 (1809).

104 "application of the coinage clause": See pp. 144–46 below.

104 " 'Historical Philology' ": Levinson 1989, 646.

104 " 'Sacred Philology' ": Kristeller 1961, 79.

104 " 'it remains one of the most momentous linguistic convergences' ": Pelikan 1993, 3.

105 " 'the Old Testament in Hebrew' ": 1.8 *Westminster Confession,* 2 Creeds 607 (1647).

105 *"editio princeps":* Amar 1987.

106 " 'Such is the character of human language' ": Chief Justice John Marshall, for the Court, *McCulloch* v. *Maryland,* 17 U.S. 414–15 (1819).

106 " 'constitution unavoidably deals in general language' ": Justice Joseph Story, *Martin* v. *Hunter's Lessee,* 14 U.S. 326–28 (1816).

106 " 'historical philology' ": Summarized in Amar 1998, 328–29 n. 5; also Kates 1983, and Bogus 2000.

106 " 'there is less agreement' ": Malcolm 1994, 135.

106 "noted earlier": See p. 39 above.

107 " 'The right . . . of "bearing arms" ' ": Chief Justice Morrison Remick Waite, for the Court, *United States* v. *Cruikshank et al.,* 92 U.S. 553 (1876).

107   " 'the amendment is a limitation' ": Justice William Burnham
       Woods, for the Court, *Presser* v. *Illinois,* 116 U.S. 265 (1886).

107   " 'The Second Amendment' ": Levy 1999, 133.

107   " 'the purpose clause' ": Williams 2003, 73.

107   "it becomes permissible to infringe' ": Hawxhurst 1991.

107   " 'the "militia" is identical to "the people" ' ": Amar 1998, 51.

107   " 'the Body of the People' ": Williams 2003, 74; capitals original.

107   " 'it is difficult to know' ": Levinson 1989, 645.

108   " " 'It is not the words of the law' " ": These words are in quota-
       tion marks in the opinion, but their source is not indicated.

108   " 'The opinion in these cases' ": Justice John Marshall Harlan,
       dissenting, *Civil Rights Cases* 109 U.S. 26 (1883).

109   " 'no one should speak' ": 14 *Tetrapolitan Confession,* 2 Creeds 234
       (1530).

109   "Constitution served as a model": Thompson 1988; Katz 1994.

109   " 'speak *only English* at school' ": Justice Oliver Wendell Holmes,
       Jr., dissenting, *Bartels* v. *Iowa,* 262 U.S. 412 (1923); italics added.

110   " 'fundamental theory of liberty' ": Justice James Clark McRey-
       nolds, for the Court, *Pierce* v. *Society of Sisters,* 268 U.S. 535 (1925).

110   " 'New York English literacy requirement' ": Justice William Jo-
       seph Brennan, Jr., for the Court, *Katzenbach* v. *Morgan,* 384 U.S.
       646–47 (1966).

110   "interpretation and translation are inseparable": Lessig 1993.

110   " 'anxiously and deliberately' ": *Ableman* v. *Booth* and *United
       States* v. *Booth,* 62 U.S. 522 (1859).

110   " 'to speak holy writ in other tongues' ": Steiner 1992, 257.

111   " 'Scriptures ought to be translated' ": 4 *Irish Articles,* 2 Creeds
       553–54 (1615).

111   " 'The Spirit has inspired' ": 6 *Reformed Church in America: Our
       Song of Hope,* 3 Creeds 788 (1978).

111   " 'We believe that the Holy Bible' ": 1–2 *New Hampshire Confes-
       sion,* 3 Creeds 243 (1833/1853); see also 7 *Statement of Faith of the
       Jehovah's Witnesses,* 3 Creeds 433 (1918).

112   " 'when vowel points' ": *ODCC* 1593.

112   " 'the student reading the verses' ": *Abington School District* v.
       Schempp, 374 U.S. 207 (1963).

113 " 'angels' refers to 'the heavenly powers' ": 2.2 *Confession of Metrophanes Critopoulos*, 1 Creeds 494 (1625).

114 "For Eastern Orthodoxy": 21 *Reponse of the Eastern Patriarchs to Pope Pius IX*, 3 Creeds 285 (1848).

114 " 'the Old Testament in Hebrew' ": 1.8 *Westminster Confession*, 2 Creeds 607 (1647).

114 " 'these entire books' ": 4.1 *Dogmatic Decrees of the Council of Trent*, 2 Creeds 823 (1546); italics added.

114 " 'the complete books of the Old and the New Testament' ": 2 *Dogmatic Constitution on the Catholic Faith of the First Vatican Council*, 3 Creeds 346 (1870); italics added.

114 " 'no translation of Holy Scripture' ": 2 *Fourteen Theses of the First Reunion Conference at Bonn*, 3 Creeds 366 (1874).

114 " 'the biblical writers *actually had in mind*' ": 22; 12 *Dogmatic Constitution on Divine Revelation*, 3 Creeds 660; 656 (1965); italics added.

4   Development of Doctrine: Patterns and Criteria

116 " 'A man who has not the most elementary' ": 1–3 *Tome of Pope Leo I*, 1 Creeds 114–15 (449).

116 " 'This is the sound tradition' ": 3 *Edict of Justinian on the True Faith*, 1 Creeds 127 (551).

116 " '*divinely inspired theological writings*' ": 23 *Tome of the Synod of Constantinople*, 1 Creeds 349 (1351); italics added.

116 " 'Following the example of the orthodox fathers' ": 4.1 *Dogmatic Decrees of the Council of Trent*, 2 Creeds 822 (1546).

116 " '*in accordance with the Scriptures*' ": 5 *Niceno-Constantinopolitan Creed*, 1 Creeds 163 (381); italics added. See also p. 9 above.

117 " '*from the tradition of the holy fathers*' ": *Formula of Union of the Council of Ephesus*, 1 Creeds 169 (431); italics added.

117 " 'just as the [Old Testament] prophets' ": 25–27 *Definition of Faith of the Council of Chalcedon*, 1 Creeds 181 (451).

117 " 'Such then are the assertions' ": 14 *Anathemas of the Second Council of Constantinople Against the Three Chapters*, 1 Creeds 213 (553).

117   " 'under God's inspiration [*theopneustōs*]' ": *Exposition of Faith of the Third Council of Constantinople*, 1 Creeds 219 (680–81).

117   " 'receive confirmation by a public decree' ": *Doctrinal Statement of the Second Council of Nicaea*, 1 Creeds 235 (787).

117   " 'anyone [who] rejects any written or unwritten tradition' ": 4 *Anathemas of the Second Council of Nicaea Concerning Holy Images*, 1 Creeds 241 (787).

118   " *'greater perhaps than any before'* ": Newman [1878] 1989, 303; italics added. See pp. 134–35 below.

118   "not an addition [*prosthēkē*]": *Formula of Union of the Council of Ephesus*, 1 Creeds 169 (431).

118   "confront all the contrary evidence": Pelikan 1990a, 41–66.

118   " 'only its great outlines should be marked' ": Chief Justice John Marshall, *McCulloch v. Maryland*, 17 U.S. 407 (1819).

118   " 'it is no answer' ": Chief Justice Charles Evans Hughes, for the Court, *Home Building and Loan Association v. Blaisdell*, 290 U.S. 442–43 (1934).

119   " 'We must recognize' ": Justice Arthur Joseph Goldberg, concurring, *New York Times Co. v. Sullivan*, 376 U.S. 299 (1964).

119   " 'We are required' ": Justice William Joseph Brennan, Jr., for the Court, *New York Times Co. v. Sullivan*, 376 U.S. 256 (1964); italics added.

119   " 'These propositions are new' ": *Ableman v. Booth* and *United States v. Booth*, 62 U.S. 514 (1859); italics added.

119   " 'an inner dimension of tradition' ": Congar 1967, 211.

120   " 'There are certain works' ": Cameron 1974, 7.

120   " 'the last print or reprint' ": Newman [1878] 1989, vi.

120   "this revised edition": Newman [1878] 1989 (I have altered the British spelling); see Bibliography.

120   "study of constitutional law": Bork 1990, 352.

120   " 'development of doctrine' ": For example, Levi 1949, 14; Gianella 1967; *OCSC* 569.

120   " 'evolving doctrine' ": Gunther 1972.

121   " 'In the case by which' ": *Credo*, 26–28.

121   " 'When we are dealing with words' ": Justice Oliver Wendell Holmes, Jr., for the Court, *Missouri v. Holland*, 252 U.S. 433 (1920).

122   " 'would violate constitutional right' ": Chief Justice Charles
      Evans Hughes, for the Court, *Near* v. *Minnesota*, 283 U.S. 717–18
      (1931).
122   " 'the whole ideal of Matthew' ": NJB on Mt 13.52.
122   " 'the sacred tradition and teaching' ": 1 *Declaration of the Second
      Vatican Council on Religious Freedom*, 3 Creeds 663 (1965).
122   " 'doctrines [which develop]' ": Newman [1878] 1989, 179.
122   " 'in mathematical creations' ": Newman [1878] 1989, 178.
123   " 'that throve and lasted' ": Newman [1878] 1989, 186.
123   " 'later councils do not formulate": Thomas Aquinas *Summa
      Theologica* 1a.36.2 (tr. Blackfriars).
123   " 'progress of the mind' ": Newman [1878] 1989, 383.
123   " 'text, tradition, and reason' ": Perry 1985.
123   " 'variations which are consistent' ": Newman [1878] 1989, 174.
123   " 'Those magistrates are called 'corrupt' ' ": Newman [1878] 1989,
      172.
123   " 'a real alteration of polity' ": Newman [1878] 1989, 176.
124   " 'Blackstone supplies us' ": Newman [1878] 1989, 202.
124   " 'Sober men are indisposed' ": Newman [1878] 1989, 203.
124   " 'pegs on which to hang a *historical* thesis' ": Chadwick 1957, 155.
124   " 'to discriminate healthy developments' ": Newman [1878] 1989,
      171.
124   " 'tokens' ": Newman [1878] 1989, 206. In citing the "notes" of
      1878 as subheads for this chapter, I have included the formulation
      of the "test" from 1845 in brackets.
124   "relation between original intent": Grey 1984, 8n.
124   " 'The development proceeds in shifts' ": Levi 1949, 59–60.
125   " 'Every calling or office' ": Newman [1878] 1989, 172.
125   " 'We cannot determine' ": Newman [1878] 1989, 176.
125   " 'More subtle still and mysterious' ": Newman [1878] 1989, 174.
125   " 'one cause of corruption' ": Newman [1878] 1989, 177.
125   " 'accuracy [*akribeia*]' ": 7 *Tome of the Synod of Constantinople*, 1
      Creeds 338 (1351).
125   "defined by the early church": Some of the material in this para-
      graph and in the one following is adapted from *Credo*, 41–43.
126   " 'believing, teaching, and maintaining' ": 10 *Reckoning of the
      Faith*, 2 Creeds 267–68 (1530).

126   " 'we confess' ": 20 *First Helvetic Confession,* 2 Creeds 288 (1536).

126   " 'We believe and confess' ": 1 *French Confession,* 2 Creeds 375 (1559/1571).

126   " 'this brief and plain confession' ": 1; 19 *Scots Confession,* 2 Creeds 389–90; 399 (1560).

126   " 'We believe with our hearts' ": *King's Confession,* 2 Creeds 542 (1581).

126   " 'We all believe in our hearts' ": 1 *Belgic Confession,* 2 Creeds 407 (1561).

126   " 'We believe and confess' ": 1.1; 3.1; 11.1; 11.11 *Second Helvetic Confession,* 2 Creeds 460; 463; 475; 477 (1566).

126   " 'We believe, teach, and confess' ": 1.1 *Formula of Concord Epitome,* 2 Creeds 168 (1577).

127   " 'I, Hans Denck, confess' ": 1 *Hans Denck's Confession Before the Council of Nuremberg,* 2 Creeds 672 (1625).

127   " 'We believe and confess' ": 2 *Dordrecht Confession,* 2 Creeds 775 (1632).

127   "principal components of faith": *The Statement of Belief of the Seventh-Day Adventist Church,* 3 Creeds 359–64 (1872).

127   "Church of Christ, Scientist": *Tenets of the Mother Church of Christ, Scientist,* 3 Creeds 370–71 (1879/1892).

127   "Mormon Church": *Articles of Faith of the Church of Jesus Christ of Latter-Day Saints,* 3 Creeds 256–58 (1842).

127   "Friends Yearly Meeting": *The Richmond Declaration of Faith,* 3 Creeds 377–92 (1887).

127   "common doctrinal faith": *The Statement of the Fundamental Truths of the Assemblies of God,* 3 Creeds 426–31 (1916).

127   " 'imposed as a creedal test' ": *Washington Profession of the Unitarian General Convention,* 3 Creeds 510 (1935).

127   " 'Thus we believe' ": 5 *The United Church of Christ in Japan,* 3 Creeds 557 (1954).

127   *"ordo iudiciorum":* 74 *Treatise on the Power and Primacy of the Pope,* 2 Creeds 162 (1537).

128   "controversy about 'incorporation' ": Curtis 1986.

128   " 'the one mass breakdown' ": Pollak 1966, 2:115.

128   " 'the words, "due process of law" ' ": Justice Benjamin Robbins

Curtis, for the Court, *Murray's Lessee* v. *Hoboken Land and Improvement Co., 59* U.S. 276 (1856).

128   " 'no longer open to doubt' ": Chief Justice Charles Evans Hughes, for the Court, *Near* v. *Minnesota,* 283 U.S. 707 (1931).

128   " 'destructive dogma against the States' ": Justice Felix Frankfurter, for the Court, *Rochin* v. *California,* 342 U.S. 168 (1952).

128   " 'due process revolution' ": *OCSC* 239.

129   " 'doctrines expand variously' ": Newman [1878] 1989, 178.

129   " 'the assumption of certain conditions' ": Newman [1878] 1989, 183.

129   " 'destruction of the special laws' ": Newman [1878] 1989, 185.

129   " 'doctrines develop' ": Newman [1878] 1989, 178–79.

129   " 'a reference to Scripture' ": Newman [1878] 1989, 339. See pp. 76–84 above.

129   " 'When developments in Christianity' ": Newman [1878] 1989, 323–24.

129   " 'particular provisions of the constitution' ": Chief Justice John Marshall, for the Court, *Fletcher* v. *Peck,* 10 U.S. 139 (1810); italics added.

130   " 'the *general principles,* which influence me' ": Justice James Iredell, *Calder* v. *Bull,* 3 U.S. 398 (1798); italics added.

130   " 'This *fundamental principle* flows' ": Justice Samuel Chase, for the Court, *Calder* v. *Bull,* 3 U.S. 388–89 (1798); italics added.

130   " *'principles of natural justice'* ": *Charles River Bridge* v. *Warren Bridge,* 36 U.S. 452–53 (1837); italics added.

130   " *'acknowledged principles of justice and equity'* ": Chief Justice Salmon Portland Chase, for the Court, *Hepburn* v. *Griswold,* 75 U.S. 607 (1869); italics added.

131   " *'principle of interpretation'* ": Justice Thomas Stanley Matthews, for the Court, *Yick Wo* v. *Hopkins,* 118 U.S. 373–74 (1886); italics added.

131   " 'Time works changes' ": Justice Joseph McKenna, for the Court, *Weems* v. *United States,* 217 U.S. 373 (1910); italics added. See also pp. 8–9 above.

131   " 'infringe *fundamental principles*": Justice Oliver Wendell Holmes, Jr., dissenting, *Lochner* v. *New York,* 198 U.S. 76 (1905); italics added. See also Sunstein 1987b.

132   " 'the very essence' ": Justice Benjamin Nathan Cardozo, for
the Court, *Palko* v. *Connecticut,* 302 U.S. 325 (1937); italics
added.

132   " 'not sports in our constitutional law' ": Justice Felix Frankfurter, for the Court, *Rochin* v. *California,* 342 U.S. 173 (1952).

132   " 'returning to these old precedents' ": Justice Hugo L. Black, for
the Court, *Gideon* v. *Wainwright,* 372 U.S. 344 (1963), against the
precedent of *Betts* v. *Brady,* 316 U.S. 455 (1942), in which he had
dissented; italics added.

132   " *'elaboration of constitutional principles'* ": Justice William Joseph
Brennan, Jr., for the Court, *New York Times Co.* v. *Sullivan,* 376
U.S. 285 (1964); italics added.

132   " 'language of the Ante-nicene fathers' ": Newman [1878] 1989,
135.

132   "confessed by both the West and the East": *Decree of the Second
Council of Lyons on the Supreme Trinity and the Catholic Faith,* 1
Creeds 744 (1274); 2 *Confession of Faith of Mark of Ephesus,* 1
Creeds 382 (1439).

132   " 'Hear, O Israel' ": *Shema,* 1 Creeds 29–31.

132   "being addressed with divine titles": Hahn 1969.

133   " 'Is the Divine that has appeared' ": Harnack [1893] 1957, 242
(translation revised).

133   " 'We believe in one God' ": 1 *Creed of Nicaea,* 1 Creeds 159 (325).

133   "the most universal of all Christian statements' ": 1 *Niceno-
Constantinopolitan Creed,* 1 Creeds 163; 672 (381).

133   " 'the Trinity, one in essence' ": II.D *Liturgy of John Chrysostom,* 1
Creeds 284.

133   " 'there is the Father' ": 2 *First London Confession,* 3 Creeds 50
(1644).

133   " 'getting rid of polytheism' ": 1 *Tome of the Synod of Constantinople,* 1 Creeds 335 (1351).

133   " 'There is only one God' ": 1 *Anathemas of the Second Council of
Constantinople,* 1 Creeds 201 (553).

134   " 'pagan multiplicity' ": 19 *Encyclical Letter of Photius,* 1 Creeds 302
(866).

134   " 'this is not the full adoration' ": *Doctrinal Statement of the Second Council of Nicaea,* 1 Creeds 237 (787).

134   " 'An eclectic, conservative, assimilating' ": Newman [1878] 1989, 186.

134   " 'the stronger and more living' ": Newman [1878] 1989, 188.

134   " 'an addition greater' ": Newman [1878] 1989, 303.

134   "interpreted . . . as the dogmatic codification": 17.8 *Confession of Faith of Metrophanes Critopoulos,* 1 Creeds 536 (1625).

135   "interpreted . . . as the *assimilation*": Jenny-Kappers 1986.

135   " 'Let us grant' ": 50 *Tome of the Synod of Constantinople,* 1 Creeds 331 (1341).

135   " 'Science is recognized' ": Arnold 1935, 730; italics added. See also Purcell 1973.

135   " 'copious collection' ": Justice David J. Brewer, for the Court, *Muller* v. *Oregon,* 208 U.S. 419 (1908); see Mason in Garraty 1975, 176–90.

135   "evidence about the functioning of juries": Kalven and Zeisel 1971.

136   " 'heredity plays an important part' ": Justice Oliver Wendell Holmes, Jr., for the Court, *Buck* v. *Bell,* 274 U.S. 206–7 (1927).

136   " 'determining the question of reasonableness' ": See Lofgren 1987.

136   " 'enforced separation of the two races' ": Justice Henry Billings Brown, for the Court, *Plessy* v. *Ferguson,* 163 U.S. 550–51 (1895).

136   " 'questionable racial and sociological grounds' ": Justice Frank Murphy, dissenting, *Korematsu* v. *United States,* 323 U.S. 236–37 (1944).

137   "a life of its own": *OCSC* 305–6.

137   "references to social science research": Chief Justice Earl Warren, for the Court, *Brown* v. *Board of Education,* 347 U.S. 494–95 (1953); see Murphy 1972, 310–14, and Kluger 1976.

137   " 'Fourth Note' ": In the version of 1845, the order of the fourth and fifth was reversed; but this sequence reflects the version of 1878.

137   " 'such intellectual processes' ": Newman [1878] 1989, 190.

137   " 'a certain continuous advance' ": Newman [1878] 1989, 195.

137   " 'one doctrine leading to another' ": Newman [1878] 1989, 383.

138   " 'truly has two natures' ": *Creed of the Synod of Rome,* 1 Creeds 724 (680).

138   " 'What man *who thinks logically*' ": 12 *Tome of the Synod of Constantinople,* 1 Creeds 342–43 (1351).

138   "creeds and confessions of the Protestant Reformation": *Credo,* 205.

138   " 'the one and the same Christ' ": 17–18 *Definition of the Council of Chalcedon,* 1 Creeds 180–81 (451).

138   "two principles of action": *Exposition of Faith of the Third Council of Constantinople,* 1 Creeds 227 (680–81).

139   " 'it does not belong to the same nature' ": 9 *Tome of Pope Leo I,* 1 Creeds 117 (449).

139   "single divine-human principle of action": *Christian Tradition,* 2: 65–66.

139   " 'two natural principles of action' ": *Third Council of Constantinople,* 1 Creeds 225 (680–81).

139   " 'the production of representational art' ": *Second Council of Nicaea,* 1 Creeds 237 (787).

139   " 'although Christ assumed human nature' ": 4.2 *Second Helvetic Confession,* 2 Creeds 464 (1566).

139   " 'either expressly set down in Scripture": 1.6 *Savoy Declaration of Faith and Order,* 3 Creeds 107 (1658).

140   " *'the logical dictate of prior cases'* ": Justice Tom Clark, for the Court, *Mapp* v. *Ohio,* 367 U.S. 657 (1960); italics added.

140   " 'particular phraseology' ": Chief Justice John Marshall, *Marbury* v. *Madison,* 5 U.S. 180 (1803); italics added.

140   " 'may be *deduced* fairly' ": Justice William Strong, for the Court, *Legal Tender Cases,* 79 U.S. 534 (1870).

140   " 'Since developments are in great measure' ": Newman [1878] 1989, 195–96.

141   " 'process by means of which' ": Congar 1972, 45.

141   " 'the name "definability" ' ": *Credo,* 1–2.

141   " 'ripeness,' or . . . 'justiciability' ": *OCSC* 737; 478.

141   " 'vague and isolated' ": Newman [1878] 1989, 195.

141   " 'in shifts' ": Levi 1949, 59–60.

141   " 'not introducing anything left out' ": *Definition of Faith of the Council of Chalcedon,* 1 Creeds 177 (451).

141   "Synod . . . of Ephesus": *Credo,* 258–59.

142   " 'not unmindful of the desirability' ": Justice Stanley Forman Reed, for the Court, *Smith* v. *Allwright,* 321 U.S. 665 (1944).

142   "unconstitutional": Justice Owen J. Roberts, for the Court, *United States* v. *Butler,* 297 U.S. 77–78 (1936).

142   "declared it to be constitutional": Justice Owen J. Roberts, for the Court, *Mulford* v. *Smith,* 307 U.S. 41–51 (1939).

142   " 'It is proper to say that' ": *Ableman* v. *Booth* and *United States* v. *Booth,* 62 U.S. 526 (1859).

142   " 'In my opinion, the judgment' ": Justice John Marshall Harlan, dissenting, *Plessy* v. *Ferguson,* 163 U.S. 559 (1896); see Lofgren 1987, 196–208.

142   " 'vague and isolated' ": Newman [1878] 1989, 195.

143   " 'A corruption' ": Newman [1878] 1989, 199.

143   " 'a true development' ": Newman [1878] 1989, 200.

143   " 'Blackstone supplies us' ": Newman [1878] 1989, 202.

143   *"preservative addition": Christian Tradition,* 2:183–98.

143   " 'We believe also' ": 3 *Rule of Faith of the Eleventh Synod of Toledo,* 1 Creeds 716–17 (675); italics added.

143   " 'we want the Holy Spirit' ": ap. 29 *Confession of Faith of Metrophanes Critopoulos,* 1 Creeds 492 (1625).

144   " 'excessive and pointless' interpolation": 8–9 *Encyclical Letter of Photius,* 1 Creeds 300–301 (866).

144   " 'contrary to the memorable declaration' ": 5 *Response of the Eastern Patriarchs to Pope Pius IX,* 3 Creeds 267–68 (1848).

144   " 'with the intention of excluding' ": 6; 9 *Decree of Union of the Council of Basel-Ferrara-Florence-Rome,* 1 Creeds 754 (1439).

144   "currency in relation to specie": Mary R. Murrin in Conley and Kaminski 1988, 59–64.

144   "discussion of the value of paper money": Johann Wolfgang von Goethe *Faust* lines 6054–6173.

144   "refers explicitly only to specie": Henry and LeFrancois 2002, 253–54.

144   " 'no lawful money of the United States' ": *Hepburn* v. *Griswold,* 75 U.S. 604; 614 (1870).

145   " 'which gives Congress power' ": Clarkson Nott Potter, *Legal Tender Cases,* 79 U.S. 464–65 (1871).

145   " 'nothing but the precious metals' ": Justice William Strong, for the Court, *Legal Tender Cases,* 79 U.S. 544 (1871).

146   " 'power to establish a standard of value' ": Chief Justice Salmon Portland Chase, for the Court, *Hepburn* v. *Griswold,* 75 U.S. 615–16 (1869).

146   " 'can Congress constitutionally give' ": Justice William Strong, for the Court, *Legal Tender Cases,* 79 U.S. 530 (1870).

146   " 'Something revived the drooping faith' ": Justice William Strong, for the Court, *Legal Tender Cases,* 79 U.S. 532–33; 541 (1870).

146   " 'there are some considerations touching' ": Justice William Strong, for the Court, *Legal Tender Cases,* 79 U.S. 545 (1870).

147   " 'the course of heresies' ": Newman [1878] 1989, 203–4; italics original.

147   " 'union of vigor with continuance' ": Newman [1878] 1989, 206.

147   " 'the holy church' ": 8–9 *Roman Symbol,* 1 Creeds 682 (2d c.).

147   " 'one, holy, catholic, and apostolic' ": 9 *Niceno-Constantinopolitan Creed,* 1 Creeds 163 (381).

148   "sacramentally, not statistically": Willis 1950, 117–18.

148   "the Reformation confessions": *Credo,* 474–76.

148   "the responses to them": 8 *Reply to the Augsburg Confession by Patriarch Jeremias II of Constantinople,* 1 Creeds 415 (1576).

148   " 'the grace which is exhibited' ": 28.3 *Savoy Declaration of Faith and Order,* 3 Creeds 127 (1658).

148   " 'union of vigor with continuance' ": Newman [1878] 1989, 206.

149   " 'When we consider the succession' ": Newman [1878] 1989, 437–38; Vergil *Aeneid* 4.175.

Bibliography

Abraham, Henry J. 1988. *Freedom and the Court: Civil Rights and Liberties in the United States.* 5th ed. New York: Oxford University Press.

Abrams, M. H. 1989. *Doing Things with Texts: Essays in Criticism and Critical Theory.* Edited by Michael Fischer. New York: W. W. Norton.

————, et al. 1972. *In Search of Literary Theory.* Edited by Morton W. Bloomfield. Ithaca, N.Y.: Cornell University Press.

Ackerman, Bruce A. 1991–98. *We the People.* 2 vols. Cambridge, Mass.: Belknap Press of Harvard University Press.

Amar, Akhil Reed. 1985. "A Neo-Federalist View of Article III: Separating the Two Tiers of Federal Jurisdiction." *Boston University Law Review* 65:205–72.

————. 1987. "Our Forgotten Constitution: A Bicentennial Comment." *Yale Law Journal* 97:281–98.

————. 1997. *The Constitution and Criminal Procedure: First Principles.* New Haven and London: Yale University Press.

————. 1998. *The Bill of Rights: Creation and Reconstruction.* New Haven and London: Yale University Press.

Anderson, J. N. D. 1959. *Islamic Law in the Modern World.* New York: New York University Press.

Arnold, Thurman W. 1935. "Apologia for Jurisprudence." *Yale Law Journal* 44:729–53.

Ascha, Ghassan. 1997. *Mariage, polygamie et répudiation en Islam: justifications des auteurs arabo-musulmans contemporains.* Paris: L'Harmattan.

Bailyn, Bernard. 1992. *The Ideological Origins of the American Revolution.* 2d ed. Cambridge, Mass.: Harvard University Press.

Ball, Terence, and J. G. A. Pocock, eds. 1988. *Conceptual Change and the Constitution.* Lawrence: University Press of Kansas.

Barnett, Randy E., ed. 1989–93. *The Rights Retained by the People: The History and Meaning of the Ninth Amendment.* 2 vols. Fairfax, Va.: George Mason University Press.

Barzun, Jacques. 1974. *The Use and Abuse of Art.* Twenty-Second Andrew W. Mellon Lectures in the Fine Arts at the National Gallery. Princeton, N.J.: Princeton University Press.

Beard, Charles Austin. 1912. *The Supreme Court and the Constitution.* New York: Macmillan.

———. [1935] 1986. *An Economic Interpretation of the Constitution of the United States.* Introduction by Forrest McDonald. New York: Free Press.

Bedau, Hugo Adam, ed. 1982. *The Death Penalty in America.* 3d ed. New York: Oxford University Press.

Beeman, Richard R., Stephen Botein, and Edward C. Carter II, eds. 1987. *Beyond Confederation: Origins of the Constitution and American National Identity.* Chapel Hill: University of North Carolina Press.

Berkson, Larry Charles. 1975. *The Concept of Cruel and Unusual Punishment.* Lexington, Mass.: Lexington Books.

Berman, Harold J. 1983. *Law and Revolution: The Formation of the Western Legal Tradition.* Cambridge, Mass.: Harvard University Press.

———. 1993. *Faith and Order: The Reconciliation of Law and Religion.* Atlanta, Ga.: Scholars Press.

Bernd, Joseph L. 1968. *Equal Protection of Voting Rights: The Logic of "One Person, One Vote."* Blacksburg: Virginia Polytechnic Institute.

Beth, Loren. 1963. "The Slaughter-House Cases—Revisited." *Louisiana Law Review* 23:487–505.

Bickel, Alexander M. [1962] 1986. *The Least Dangerous Branch*. 2d ed. Foreword by Harry H. Wellington. New Haven and London: Yale University Press.

———. 1978. *The Supreme Court and the Idea of Progress*. Foreword by Anthony Lewis. New Haven and London: Yale University Press.

———, and Benno C. Schmidt, Jr. 1984. *The Judiciary and Responsible Government, 1910–21*. New York: Macmillan.

Black, Charles L., Jr. 1969. *Structure and Relationship in Constitutional Law*. Baton Rouge: Louisiana State University Press.

Black, Hugo LaFayette. 1968. *A Constitutional Faith*. The James S. Carpentier Lectures for 1968. With a foreword by William C. Warren. New York: Alfred A. Knopf.

Blanc, François-Paul. 1995. *Le droit musulman*. Paris: Dalloz.

Blaustein, Albert P., ed. 1992. *The Bicentennial Concordance: Indexes to the Constitution of the United States of America*. Littleton, Colo.: Rothman.

Bobbitt, Philip. 1982. *Constitutional Fate: Theory of the Constitution*. New York: Oxford University Press.

———. 1991. *Constitutional Interpretation*. Cambridge, Mass.: B. Blackwell.

Bogus, Carl T., ed. 2000. *The Second Amendment in Law and History: Historians and Constitutional Scholars on the Right to Bear Arms*. New York: New Press.

Bollinger, Lee C. 1991. *Images of a Free Press*. Chicago: University of Chicago Press.

Boorstin, Daniel J. [1941] 1996. *The Mysterious Science of the Law: An Essay on Blackstone's Commentaries*. With a new foreword. Chicago: University of Chicago Press.

Bork, Robert H. 1991. *The Tempting of America: The Political Seduction of the Law*. 2d ed. Afterword by the author. New York: Simon and Schuster.

Bousset, Wilhelm. 1915. *Jüdisch-christlicher Schulbetrieb in Alexandria und Rom: Literarische Untersuchungen zu Philo und Clemens von Alexandria, Justin und Irenäus*. Göttingen: Vandenhoeck und Ruprecht.

Bradford, M. E. 1993. *Original Intentions: On the Making and Ratification of the United States Constitution*. Athens: University of Georgia Press.

Brennan, William Joseph, Jr. 1967. *An Affair with Freedom: A Collection of His Opinions and Speeches Drawn from His First Decade as a United States Supreme Court Justice*. Edited by Stephen J. Friedman. Foreword by Arthur J. Goldberg. New York: Atheneum.

Brest, Paul. 1980. "The Misconceived Quest for the Original Understanding." *Boston University Law Review* 60:204–38.

———. 1982. "Interpretation and Interest." *Stanford Law Review* 34: 765–73.

———, and Sanford Levinson. 2000. *Processes of Constitutional Decision-Making*. 4th ed. Gaithersburg, Md.: Aspen Law and Business.

Brigham, John. 1978. *Constitutional Language: An Interpretation of Judicial Decisions*. Westport, Conn.: Greenwood Press.

———. 1987. *The Cult of the Court*. Philadelphia: Temple University Press.

Brown, Raymond Edward. 1955. *The Sensus Plenior of Sacred Scripture*. Baltimore: Saint Mary's University.

Burt, Robert A. 1984. "Constitutional Law and the Teaching of the Parables." *Yale Law Journal* 93:455–502.

Butterfield, Herbert. 1931. *The Whig Interpretation of History*. London: Bell.

Cahn, Edmond Nathaniel. 1966. *Confronting Injustice: The Edmond Cahn Reader*. Edited by Lenore L. Cahn. Foreword by Hugo L. Black. Introduction and notes by Norman Redlich. Boston: Little, Brown.

———. 1981. *The Moral Decision: Right and Wrong in the Light of*

American Law. New Midland Book ed. Bloomington: Indiana University Press.

———, ed. 1954. *Supreme Court and Supreme Law.* Bloomington: Indiana University Press.

Cameron, James Munro. 1974. "Editor's Introduction." In John Henry Newman, *An Essay on the Development of Christian Doctrine* (1845), 7–50. Reprint edition. Harmondsworth: Penguin Classics.

Cardozo, Benjamin N. [1921] 1960. *The Nature of the Judicial Process.* New Haven: Yale University Press.

Carter, Stephen. 1987. "Evolutionism, Creationism, and Treating Religion as a Hobby." *Duke Law Journal* 1987:977–96.

Casper, Gerhard. 1989. "Changing Concepts of Constitutionalism: Eighteenth to Twentieth Century." *Supreme Court Review* 1989:311–32.

Chadwick, Owen. 1957. *From Bossuet to Newman: The Idea of Doctrinal Development.* Cambridge: Cambridge University Press.

Chaudrhy, Muhammad Sharif. 1997. *Code of Islamic Laws: The Criminal and Civic Laws of Islam Directly Deduced from the Qur'an.* Lahore: Impact Publications International.

Chenu, Marie-Dominique. 1964. *Toward Understanding Saint Thomas.* Translated by A.-M. Landry and D. Hughes. Chicago: Henry Regnery.

Choper, Jesse H. 1980. *Judicial Review and the National Political Process: A Functional Reconsideration of the Role of the Supreme Court.* Chicago: University of Chicago Press.

———. 1995. *Securing Religious Liberty: Principles for Judicial Interpretation of the Religion Clauses.* Chicago: University of Chicago Press.

Clark, Floyd Barzilia. 1915. *The Constitutional Doctrines of Justice Harlan.* Baltimore: Johns Hopkins Press.

Clinton, Robert Lowry. 1989. *Marbury v. Madison and Judicial Review.* Lawrence: University Press of Kansas.

Congar, Yves M.-J. 1967. *Tradition and Traditions: An Historical and a Theological Essay.* Translated by Michael Naseby and Thomas Rainborough. New York: Macmillan.

———. 1972. "Reception as an Ecclesiological Reality." In Giuseppe Alberigo and Anton Weiler, eds., *Election and Consensus in the Church*, 43–68. New York: Herder and Herder.

———. 1976. "Pour une histoire sémantique du terme *magisterium*"; "Bref historique des formes du 'magistère' et de ses relations avec les docteurs." *Revue des sciences philosophiques et théologiques* 60:85–112.

Conley, Patrick T., and John P. Kaminski, eds. 1988. *The Constitution and the States: The Role of the Original Thirteen in the Framing and Adoption of the Federal Constitution.* Madison, Wis.: Madison House.

———. 1992. *The Bill of Rights and the States: The Colonial and Revolutionary Origins of American Liberties.* Madison, Wis.: Madison House.

Cook, Michael A. 1981. *Early Muslim Dogma: A Source-Critical Study.* Cambridge: Cambridge University Press.

———. 2000. *Commanding Right and Forbidding Wrong in Islamic Thought.* Cambridge: Cambridge University Press.

Cooke, Jacob E., ed. 1961. *The Federalist.* Middletown, Conn.: Wesleyan University Press.

Corwin, Edward Samuel. 1920. *The Constitution and What It Means Today.* Princeton, N.J.: Princeton University Press.

———. 1959. *The "Higher Law" Background of American Constitutional Law.* Ithaca, N.Y.: Cornell University Press.

———. 1981. *Corwin on the Constitution.* Edited by Richard Loss. Ithaca, N.Y.: Cornell University Press.

Cover, Robert M. 1975. *Justice Accused: Anti-Slavery and the Judicial Process.* New Haven and London: Yale University Press.

———. 1983. " 'Nomos' and Narrative." *Harvard Law Review* 97:4–68.

Currie, David P. 1985. *The Constitution in the Supreme Court: The First*

Hundred Years, 1789–1888. Chicago: University of Chicago Press.

Curtis, Michael Kent. 1986. *No State Shall Abridge: The Fourteenth Amendment and the Bill of Rights.* Durham, N.C.: Duke University Press.

Dahl, Robert A. 1957. "Decision-Making in a Democracy: The Supreme Court as a National Policy Maker." In Hall 2001, 117–33.

Daniélou, Jean. 1960. *From Shadows to Reality: Studies in the Biblical Typology of the Fathers.* Translated by Wulstan Hibberd. Westminster, Md.: Newman Press.

Daube, David. 1969. *Studies in Biblical Law.* New York: Ktav Publishing House.

Dellinger, Walter. 1983. "The Legitimacy of Constitutional Change: Rethinking the Amending Process." *Harvard Law Review* 97: 386–432.

DeLubac, Henri. 1998–2000. *Medieval Exegesis.* Translated by Mark Sebane. 2 vols. Grand Rapids, Mich.: Wm. B. Eerdmans Publishing House.

Dorsen, Norman, ed. 1987. *The Evolving Constitution: Essays on the Bill of Rights and the U.S. Supreme Court.* Introduction by Archibald Cox. Middletown, Conn.: Wesleyan University Press.

————. 2002. *The Unpredictable Constitution.* New York: New York University Press.

DuBois, W. E. B. [1903] 1990. *The Souls of Black Folk.* Introduction by John Edgar Wideman. Library of America edition. New York: Vintage Books.

Dworkin, Ronald M. 1996. *Freedom's Law: The Moral Reading of the American Constitution.* Cambridge, Mass.: Harvard University Press.

Ebeling, Gerhard. 1947. *Kirchengeschichte als Geschichte der Auslegung der Heiligen Schrift.* Tübingen: J. C. B. Mohr (Paul Siebeck).

Edge, Ian, ed. 1996. *Islamic Law and Legal Theory*. New York: New York University Press.

Elert, Werner. 1962. *The Structure of Lutheranism*. Translated by Walter A. Hansen. Foreword by Jaroslav Pelikan. Saint Louis, Mo.: Concordia Publishing House.

Ely, John Hart. 1980. *Democracy and Distrust: A Theory of Judicial Review*. Cambridge, Mass.: Harvard University Press.

Emerson, Ralph Waldo. 1992. *The Selected Writings of Ralph Waldo Emerson*. Edited by Brooks Atkinson. New York: Modern Library.

Epstein, Richard A. 1985. *Takings: Private Property and the Power of Eminent Domain*. Cambridge, Mass.: Harvard University Press.

————. 1992. "A Common Lawyer Looks at Constitutional Interpretation." *Boston University Law Review* 72:699–727.

Eskridge, William N., Jr. 1994. *Dynamic Statutory Interpretation*. Cambridge, Mass.: Harvard University Press.

————, ed, with Sanford Levinson. 1998. *Constitutional Stupidities, Constitutional Tragedies*. New York: New York University Press.

Fallon, Richard H., Jr. 1987. "A Constructivist Coherence Theory of Constitutional Interpretation." *Harvard Law Review* 100:1189–1286.

Farber, Daniel A., and Suzanna Sherry. 2002. *Desperately Seeking Certainty: The Misguided Quest for Constitutional Foundations*. Chicago: University of Chicago Press.

Fehrenbacher, Don Edward. 1978. *The Dred Scott Case: Its Significance in American Law and Politics*. New York: Oxford University Press.

Fish, Stanley E. 1980. *Is There a Text in This Class? The Authority of Interpretive Communities*. Cambridge, Mass.: Harvard University Press.

————. 1989. *Doing What Comes Naturally: Change, Rhetoric, and the*

Practice of Theory in Literary and Legal Studies. Durham, N.C.:
Duke University Press.

Fisher, Louis. 1997. *Constitutional Conflicts Between Congress and the
President*. 4th ed. Lawrence: University Press of Kansas.

———. 2001. *American Constitutional Law*. 4th ed. Durham, N.C.:
Carolina Academic Press.

Fiss, Owen. 1982. "Objectivity and Interpretation." *Stanford Law Review* 34:739–63.

Frankfurter, Felix. 1970. *Law and Politics: Occasional Papers of Felix
Frankfurter, 1913–1938*. Edited by Archibald MacLeish and E.
F. Pritchard, Jr. New York: Harcourt, Brace.

Freedman, David Noel, ed. 1992 *The Anchor Bible Dictionary*. 6 vols.
New York: Doubleday.

Freyer, Tony Allan. 1990. *Hugo L. Black and the Dilemma of American
Liberalism*. Edited by Oscar Handlin. Glenview, Ill.: Scott,
Foresman / Little, Brown Higher Education.

Frye, Northrop. 1982. *Great Code: The Bible and Literature*. New
York: Harcourt Brace Jovanovich.

Garet, Ronald R. 1985. "Comparative Normative Hermeneutics:
Scripture, Literature, Constitution." *Southern California Law
Review* 58:35–134.

Garraty, John, ed. 1987. *Quarrels That Have Shaped the Constitution*.
New York: Harper and Row.

Gianella, Donald A. 1967–68. "Religious Liberty, Nonestablishment,
and Doctrinal Development." *Harvard Law Review* 80:1381–
1431; 81:513–90.

Gillette, William. 1969. *The Right to Vote: Politics and the Passage of
the Fifteenth Amendment*. Baltimore: Johns Hopkins University Press.

Gilmore, Grant. 1977. *The Ages of American Law*. Storrs Lectures for
1974. New Haven and London: Yale University Press.

Goebel, Julius, Jr. 1971–88. *History of the Supreme Court of the United
States*. 9 vols. New York: Macmillan.

Greene, Thurston, et al., eds. 1991. *The Language of the Constitution: A Sourcebook and Guide to the Ideas, Terms, and Vocabulary Used by the Framers of the United States Constitution*. Westport, Conn.: Greenwood Press.

Grey, Thomas C. 1984. "The Constitution as Scripture." *Stanford Law Review* 37:1–25.

Grimes, Alan Pendleton. 1978. *Democracy and the Amendments to the Constitution*. Lexington, Mass.: Lexington Books.

Grossberg, Michael. 1985. *Governing the Hearth: Law and the Family in Nineteenth-Century America*. Chapel Hill: University of North Carolina Press.

Gunther, Gerald. 1972. "Foreword: In Search of Evolving Doctrine on a Changing Court: A Model for a Newer Equal Protection." *Harvard Law Review* 86:1–48.

Hahn, Ferdinand. 1969. *Titles of Jesus in Christology: Their History in Early Christianity*. Translated by Harold Knight and George Ogg. New York: World Publishing.

Haines, Charles Grove. 1930. *The Revival of Natural Law Concepts*. Cambridge, Mass.: Harvard University Press.

Hall, Kermit L. 1987. *The Formation and Ratification of the Constitution*. New York: Garland Publishing.

———, ed. 1992. *The Oxford Companion to the Supreme Court of the United States*. New York: Oxford University Press.

———. 2001. *The Supreme Court in American Society: Equal Justice Under Law*. New York: Garland Publishing.

Hand, Learned. 1958. *The Bill of Rights*. The Oliver Wendell Holmes Lectures. Cambridge, Mass.: Harvard University Press.

Harnack, Adolf. [1893] 1957. *Outlines of the History of Dogma*. Translated by Edwin Knox Mitchell. Reprint edition. Introduction by Philip Rieff. Boston: Starr King Press.

Harris, William F., II. 1993. *The Interpretable Constitution*. Baltimore: Johns Hopkins University Press.

Hauser, Alan J., and Duane E. Watson, eds. 2002. *A History of Bib-*

lical Interpretation. Grand Rapids, Mich.: Wm. B. Eerdmans Publishing House.

Hawxhurst, Joan C. 1991. *The Second Amendment.* Introduction by Warren E. Burger. Englewood Cliffs, N.J.: Silver Burdett Press.

Henry, Robert H., and Arthur G. LeFrancois. 2002. "Liberalism, the Constitution, and the Supreme Court." In Martin H. Belsky, ed., *The Rehnquist Court: A Retrospective,* 253–73. New York: Oxford University Press.

al-Hibri, Azizah Y. 2001. "Redefining Muslim Women's Roles in the Next Century." In Norman Dorsen and Prosser Gifford, eds., *Democracy and the Rule of Law,* 90–100. Washington, D.C.: CQ Press.

Himmelfarb, Gertrude. 1987. *The New History and the Old.* Cambridge, Mass.: Harvard University Press.

Holmes, Oliver Wendell, Jr. 1881. *The Common Law.* London: Macmillan.

———. 1899. "The Theory of Legal Interpretation." *Harvard Law Review* 12:417–20.

Houtepen, Anton, ed. 1995. *The Living Tradition: Towards an Ecumenical Hermeneutics of the Christian Tradition.* Utrecht: Interuniversitair Instituut voor Missiologie en Oecumenica.

Huizing, Petrus, and Knut Walf. 1983. *The Ecumenical Council: Its Significance in the Constitution of the Church.* Edinburgh: T. and T. Clark.

Hutson, James H. 1998. *Religion and the Founding of the American Republic.* Foreword by Jaroslav Pelikan. Washington, D.C.: Library of Congress.

Issacharoff, Samuel, Pamela S. Karlan, and Richard H. Pildes. 2001. *The Law of Democracy: Legal Structure of the Political Process.* 2d ed. Westbury, N.Y.: Foundation Press.

Jenny-Kappers, Theodora. 1986. *Muttergöttin und Gottesmutter in Ephesos: Von Artemis zu Maria.* Zurich: Daimon.

Joheir, Hussein Moussa. 1983. *Polygamie et condition de la femme dans l'Islam*. Dakar: Nouvelles éditions africaines.

Jones, Arnold Hugh Martin. 1966. *Were Ancient Heresies Disguised Social Movements?* Philadelphia: Fortress Press.

Kahn, Ronald. 1989. "Polity and Rights Values in Conflict: The Burger Court, Ideological Interests, and the Separation of Church and State." *Studies in American Political Development: An Annual* 3:279–93.

Kalven, Harry, Jr. 1964. "The New York Times Case: A Note on 'The Central Meaning of the First Amendment.'" *Supreme Court Review* 1964:191–221.

———, and Hans Zeisel. 1971. *The American Jury*. Chicago: University of Chicago Press.

Kaminski, John P., and Richard Leffler, eds. 1999. *Creating the Constitution*. Acton, Mass.: Copley Publishing Group.

Kates, D. B., Jr. 1983. "Handgun Prohibition and the Original Meaning of the Second Amendment." *Michigan Law Review* 82: 204–73.

Katz, Stanley N. 1994. *Constitutionalism in East Central Europe: Some Negative Lessons from the American Experience*. Providence, R.I.: Berghahn Books.

King, Michael, ed. 1995. *God's Law Versus State Law: The Construction of an Islamic Identity in Western Europe*. London: Grey Seal.

Kirkpatrick, Ralph. 1984. *Interpreting Bach's "Well-Tempered Clavier": A Performer's Discourse of Method*. New Haven and London: Yale University Press.

Kluger, Richard. 1976. *Simple Justice: The History of Brown v. Board of Education and Black America's Struggle for Equality*. New York: Knopf.

Krausz, Michael, ed. 2002. *Is There a Single Right Interpretation?* University Park: Pennsylvania State University Press.

Kriele, Martin, et al. 1999. *Interpretation des Heiligen: Interpretation des Rechts*. Münster: LIT.

Kristeller, Paul Oskar. 1961. *Renaissance Thought: The Classic, Scholastic, and Humanist Strains.* New York: Harper Torchbooks.

Kurland, Philip B. 1978. *Watergate and the Constitution.* Chicago: University of Chicago Press.

Kutler, Stanley I, ed. 1967. *The Dred Scot Decision: Law or Politics?* Boston: Houghton Mifflin.

LaFave, Wayne R. 1986. "The Forgotten Motto of Obsta Principiis in Fourth Amendment Jurisprudence." *Arizona Law Review* 28:291–310.

Lasser, William. 1985. "The Supreme Court in Periods of Critical Realignment." *Journal of Politics* 47:1174–87.

Leclercq, Jean. 1982. *The Love of Learning and the Desire for God: A Study of Monastic Culture.* Translated by Catharine Misrahi. 3d ed. New York: Mentor Omega.

Ledwon, Lenora, ed. 1996. *Law and Literature: Text and Theory.* New York: Garland.

Leinsdorf, Erich. 1981. *The Composer's Advocate: A Radical Orthodoxy for Musicians.* New Haven and London: Yale University Press.

Lerner, Max. 1937. "Constitution and Court as Symbols." *Yale Law Journal* 46:1290–1319.

Lessig, Lawrence. 1993. "The Fidelity in Translation." *Texas Law Review* 71:1165–1268.

Levi, Edward Hirsch. 1949. *An Introduction to Legal Reasoning.* Chicago: University of Chicago Press.

Levinson, Sanford. 1979. " 'The Constitution' in American Civil Religion." *Supreme Court Review* 123.

———. 1989. "The Embarrassing Second Amendment." *Yale Law Journal* 99:637–59.

———, and Steven Mailloux, eds. 1988. *Interpreting Law and Literature: A Hermeneutic Reader.* Evanston, Ill.: Northwestern University Press.

Levy, Leonard W. 1988. *Original Intent and the Framers' Constitution.* New York: Macmillan.

———. 1993. *Blasphemy: Verbal Offense Against the Sacred, from Moses to Salman Rushdie*. New York: Alfred A. Knopf.

———. 1994. *The Establishment Clause: Religion and the First Amendment*. 2d ed. Chapel Hill: University of North Carolina Press.

———. 1999. *Origins of the Bill of Rights*. New Haven and London: Yale University Press.

Lieber, Francis. 1880. *Legal and Political Hermeneutics, or Principles of Interpretation and Construction in Law and Politics, with Remarks on Precedents and Authorities*. 3d ed. Saint Louis, Mo.: F. H. Thomas.

Lintott, Andrew William. 1999. *The Constitution of the Roman Republic*. Oxford: Clarendon Press.

Llewellyn, Karl Nickerson. 1960. *The Common-Law Tradition: Deciding Appeals*. Boston: Little, Brown.

Lofgren, Charles A. 1980. "The Origins of the Tenth Amendment: History, Sovereignty, and the Problem of Constitutional Intention." In Ronald K. L. Collins, ed., *Constitutional Government in America*, 331–57. Durham, N.C.: Carolina Academic Press.

———. 1987. *The Plessy Case: A Legal-Historical Interpretation*. New York: Oxford University Press.

McCann, Michael W., and Gerald L. Houseman, ed. 1989. *Judging the Constitution: Critical Essays on Judicial Lawmaking*. Glenview, Ill.: Scott, Foresman.

McConnell, Michael W., Robert F. Cochran, Jr., and Angela C. Carmella, eds. 2001. *Christian Perspectives on Legal Thought*. New Haven and London: Yale University Press.

Mackey, Louis. 1999. *Peregrinations of the Word*. Ann Arbor: University of Michigan Press.

Maier, Pauline. 1997. *American Scripture: Making the Declaration of Independence*. New York: Alfred A. Knopf.

Malcolm, Joyce Lee. 1994. *To Keep and Bear Arms: The Origins of an Anglo-American Right*. Cambridge, Mass.: Harvard University Press.

Marshall, Robert Lewis. 1972. *The Compositional Process of J. S. Bach: A Study of the Autograph Scores of the Vocal Works*. 2 vols. Princeton, N.J.: Princeton University Press.

Marshall, Thurgood. 1987. "Reflections on the Bicentennial of the United States Constitution." *Harvard Law Review* 101: 1–5.

Matter, E. Ann. 1990. *The Voice of My Beloved: The Song of Songs in Western Medieval Christianity*. Philadelphia: University of Pennsylvania Press.

Menand, Louis. 2001. *The Metaphysical Club*. New York: Farrar, Straus and Giroux.

Moeller, John. 1985. "Alexander Bickel: Toward a Theory of Politics." *Journal of Politics* 17:113–39.

Moldaenke, Günter. 1936. *Schriftverständnis und Schriftdeutung im Zeitalter der Reformation*. Stuttgart: W. Kohlhammer.

Murphy, Paul L. 1972. *The Constitution in Crisis Times, 1918–1969*. New York: Harper and Row.

Nagel, Robert F. 1985. "The Formulaic Constitution." *Michigan Law Review* 84:165–212.

Newman, John Henry. [1859] 1962. *On Consulting the Faithful in Matters of Doctrine*. Edited by John Coulson. New York: Sheed and Ward.

———. [1864] 1967. *Apologia pro vita sua: Being a History of His Religious Opinions*. Edited by Martin J. Svaglic. Oxford: Clarendon Press.

———. [1878] 1989. *An Essay on the Development of Christian Doctrine*. 2d ed. Reprint. Introduction by Ian Ker. Notre Dame, Ind.: University of Notre Dame Press.

Newmeyer, R. Kent. 1985. *Supreme Court Justice Joseph Story: Statesman of the Old Republic*. Chapel Hill: University of North Carolina Press.

Noonan, John T. 1987. *The Believer and the Powers That Are: Cases, History, and Other Data Bearing on the Relation of Religion and Government*. New York: Macmillan.

————. 2001. *Religious Freedom: History, Cases, and Other Materials on the Interaction of Religion and Government.* New York: Foundation Press.

Norris, Frederick W. 1978. "Apostolic, Catholic, and Sensible: The *Consensus Fidelium.*" In C. Robert Wetzel, ed., *Essays on New Testament Christianity,* 15–29. Cincinnati, Ohio: Standard Publishing.

O'Connor, John E. 1979. *William Paterson Lawyer and Statesman, 1745–1806.* New Brunswick, N.J.: Rutgers University Press.

Patterson, James T. 2001. *Brown v Board of Education: A Civil Rights Milestone and Its Troubled Legacy.* New York: Oxford University Press.

Pelikan, Jaroslav. 1946. "Luther and the *Confessio Bohemica.*" Ph.D. diss., University of Chicago.

————. 1952. "In memoriam: Johann Albrecht Bengel, June 24, 1687 to November 2, 1752." *Concordia Theological Monthly* 23:785–96.

————. 1959. *Luther the Expositor: Introduction to the Reformer's Exegetical Writings.* Companion volume to *Luther's Works.* Saint Louis, Mo.: Concordia Publishing House.

————. 1967. "Verius servamus canones: Church Law and Divine Law in the Apology of the Augsburg Confession." In *Studia Gratiana* 11 (1967), special issue, *Collectanea Stephan Kuttner,* edited by Alphons M. Stickler, 1:367–88.

————. 1971–89. *The Christian Tradition: A History of the Development of Doctrine.* 5 vols. Chicago: University of Chicago Press.

————. 1984. "Some Uses of Apocalypse in the Magisterial Reformers." In C. A. Patrides and Joseph Wittreich, eds., *The Apocalypse in English Renaissance Thought and Literature: Patterns, Antecedents, and Repercussions,* 74–92. Ithaca, N.Y.: Cornell University Press, 1984.

————. 1990a. *Imago Dei: The Byzantine Apologia for Icons.* The Andrew W. Mellon Lectures in the Fine Arts for 1987. Princeton, N.J.: Princeton University Press.

————. 1990b. "Canonica regula: The Trinitarian Hermeneutics of

Augustine." In Joseph C. Schnaubel and Frederick Van Fleteren, eds., *Collectanea Augustiniana,* I, *Augustine: "Second Founder of the Faith,"* 329–43. New York: Lang.

———. 1992. *On Searching the Scriptures, Your Own or Someone Else's.* Companion Guide to *Sacred Writings.* New York: History Book Club.

———. 1993. *Christianity and Classical Culture: The Metamorphosis of Natural Theology in the Christian Encounter with Hellenism.* Gifford Lectures at Aberdeen for 1992–93. New Haven and London: Yale University Press.

———. 1996. *The Reformation of the Bible / The Bible of the Reformation.* With Valerie R. Hotchkiss and David Price. New Haven and London: Yale University Press.

———. 1997. *What Has Athens to Do with Jerusalem? "Timaeus" and "Genesis" in Counterpoint.* Ann Arbor: University of Michigan Press.

———. 2001. *Divine Rhetoric: The Sermon on the Mount as Message and as Model in Augustine, Chrysostom, and Luther.* Crestwood, N.Y.: Saint Vladimir's Seminary Press.

———. 2003. *Credo: Historical and Theological Introduction to Creeds and Confessions of Faith in the Christian Tradition.* New Haven and London: Yale University Press.

———, ed., with Valerie Hotchkiss. 2003. *Creeds and Confessions of Faith in the Christian Tradition.* 3 vols. New Haven and London: Yale University Press.

Peltason, Jack W. 1994. *Understanding the Constitution.* 13th ed. Fort Worth, Tex.: Harcourt Brace College Publishers.

Perry, Michael J. 1982. *The Constitution, the Courts, and Human Rights: An Inquiry into the Legitimacy of Constitutional Policy-Making by the Judiciary.* New Haven and London: Yale University Press.

———. 1985. "The Authority of Text, Tradition, and Reason: A Theory of Constitutional Interpretation." *Southern California Law Review* 58:551–602.

Piepkorn, Arthur Carl. 1993. *The Church: Selected Writings of Arthur Carl Piepkorn*. Edited by Michael P. Plekon and William S. Wiecher. Afterword by Richard John Neuhaus. Delhi, N.Y.: ALPB Books.

Plaskin, Glenn. 1983. *Horowitz: A Biography of Vladimir Horowitz*. New York: William Morrow.

Polenberg, Richard. 1987. *Fighting Faiths: The Abrams Case, the Supreme Court, and Free Speech*. New York: Viking Books.

Pollak, Louis H. 1966. *The Constitution and the Supreme Court: A Documentary History*. 2 vols. Cleveland: World Publishing.

Pool, Ithiel de Sola. 1983. *Technologies of Freedom*. Cambridge, Mass.: Belknap Press of Harvard University Press.

Posner, Richard A. 1998. *Law and Literature*. 2d ed. Cambridge, Mass.: Harvard University Press.

———. 1999. *The Problematics of Moral and Legal Theory*. Cambridge, Mass.: Harvard University Press.

Powell, H. Jefferson. 1985. "The Original Understanding of Original Intent." *Harvard Law Review* 98:885–948.

———. 1993. *The Moral Tradition of American Constitutionalism: A Theological Interpretation*. Durham, N.C.: Duke University Press.

Purcell, Edward A., Jr. 1973. *The Crisis of Democratic Theory: Scientific Naturalism and the Problem of Value*. Lexington: University Press of Kentucky.

Rabban, David M. 1981. "The First Amendment in Its Forgotten Years." *Yale Law Journal* 90:514–95.

———. 1983. "The Emergence of Modern First Amendment Doctrine." *University of Chicago Law Review* 50:1205–1355.

Rahe, Paul A. 1992. *Republics Ancient and Modern: Classical Republicanism and the American Revolution*. Chapel Hill: University of North Carolina Press.

Rakove, Jack N. 1996. *Original Meanings: Politics and Ideas in the Making of the Constitution*. New York: Alfred A. Knopf.

Reid, Charles J. 1991. "The Canonistic Contribution to the Western Rights Tradition." *Boston College Law Review* 33:37–92.

Richards, David A. J. 1983. "The Aims of Constitutional Theory." *University of Dayton Law Review* 8:723–44.

Rockwood, Bruce, ed. 1998. *Law and Literature Perspectives*. New York: Peter Lang.

Sadat, Jihan. 1987. *A Woman of Egypt*. London: Bloomsbury.

Schauer, Frederick. 1979. "Speech and 'Speech'—Obscenity and 'Obscenity': An Exercise in the Interpretation of Constitutional Language." *Georgetown Law Journal* 67:899–933.

Schwartz, Bernard. 1973. *From Confederation to Nation: The American Constitution, 1837–1877*. Baltimore: Johns Hopkins University Press.

Sherry, Suzanna. 1987. "The Founders' Unwritten Constitution." *University of Chicago Law Review* 54:1127–77.

Shiffrin, Steven. 1983. "The First Amendment and Economic Regulation: Away from a General Theory of the First Amendment." *Northwestern Law Review* 78:1212–83.

Smith, Rodney K. 1987. *Public Prayer and the Constitution: A Case Study in Constitutional Interpretation*. Wilmington, Del.: Scholarly Resources.

Steiner, George. 1992. *After Babel: Aspects of Language and Translation*. 2d ed. New York: Oxford University Press.

Story, Joseph. [1833] 1994. *Commentaries on the Constitution of the United States*. 5th ed. Edited by Melville M. Bigelow. 2 vols. Buffalo, N.Y.: William S. Hein.

Stravinsky, Igor, and Robert Craft. 1981. *Expositions and Developments*. Paperback edition. Berkeley: University of California Press.

Sunstein, Cass R. 1987a. "Constitutionalism After the New Deal." *Harvard Law Review* 101:422–510.

———. 1987b. "*Lochner*'s Legacy." *Columbia Law Review* 87:873–919.

Swindler, William Finley. 1969–74. *Court and Constitution in the Twentieth Century*. 3 vols. Indianapolis, Ind.: Bobbs-Merrill.

———. 1978. *The Constitution and Chief Justice Marshall*. Introduction by Warren E. Burger. New York: Dodd, Mead.

Thayer, James Bradley. 1893. "The Origin and Scope of the American Doctrine of Constitutional Law." *Harvard Law Review* 7:129–56.

Thompson, Kenneth W., ed. 1988. *The U.S. Constitution and the Constitutions of Asia*. Charlottesville, Va.: Miller Center of the University of Virginia.

Tierney, Brian. 1982. *Religion, Law, and the Growth of Constitutional Thought: 1150–1650*. Cambridge: Cambridge University Press.

———. 1998. *Foundations of the Conciliar Theory: The Contributions of the Medieval Canonists from Gratian to the Great Schism*. 2d ed. Leiden: E. J. Brill.

Toorn, Pieter C. van den. 1983. *The Music of Igor Stravinsky*. New Haven and London: Yale University Press.

Tribe, Laurence H. 1985. *Constitutional Choices*. Cambridge, Mass.: Harvard University Press.

———. 1992. *Abortion: The Clash of Absolutes*. 2d ed. New York: W. W. Norton.

———, and Michael C. Dorf. 1991. *On Reading the Constitution*. Cambridge, Mass.: Harvard University Press.

Tushnet, Mark V. 1983. "Following the Rules Laid Down: A Critique of Interpretivism and Neutral Principles." *Harvard Law Review* 96:781–827.

———. 1988. *Red, White, and Blue: A Critical Analysis of Constitutional Law*. Cambridge, Mass.: Harvard University Press.

Ullmann, Walter. 1949. *Medieval Papalism: The Political Theories of the Medieval Canonists*. London: Methuen.

Vergin, Nur. 2001. "Secular State and Muslim Society: The Case of Turkey." In Norman Dorsen and Prosser Gifford, eds., *De-*

mocracy and the Rule of Law, 270–82. Washington, D.C.: CQ Press.

Vetter, Helmuth, and Michael Potacs, eds. 1990. *Beiträge zur juristischen Hermeneutik.* Vienna: Literas.

Vlad, Roman. 1960. *Stravinsky.* Translated by Frederick and Ann Fuller. London: Oxford University Press.

Vögele, Wolfgang. 2000. *Menschenwürde zwischen Recht und Theologie: Begründungen von Menschenrechten in der Perspektive öffentlicher Theologie.* Gütersloh: Christian Kaiser / Gütersloher Verlagshaus.

Ward, Ian. 1995. *Law and Literature: Possibilities and Perspectives.* New York: Cambridge University Press.

Washington, James Melvin, ed. 1986. *A Testament of Hope: The Essential Writings of Martin Luther King, Jr.* New York: Harper and Row.

Wechsler, Herbert. 1959. "Toward Neutral Principles of Constitutional Law." *Harvard Law Review* 73:1–35.

Wellington, Harry H. 1983. "History and Morals in Constitutional Adjudication." *Harvard Law Review* 97:326–35.

Westin, Alan F. 1958. *The Anatomy of a Constitutional Law Case: Youngstown Sheet and Tube Co. v. Sawyer; The Steel Seizure Decision.* New York: Macmillan.

White, G. Edward. 2000. *The Constitution and the New Deal.* Cambridge, Mass.: Harvard University Press.

Williams, David C. 2003. *The Mythic Meanings of the Second Amendment: Taming Political Violence in a Constitutional Republic.* New Haven and London: Yale University Press.

Willis, Geoffrey Grimshaw. 1950. *Saint Augustine and the Donatist Controversy.* London: S.P.C.K.

Wimsatt, Wiliam K., Jr. 1954. *Verbal Icon: Studies in the Meaning of Poetry.* Lexington: University of Kentucky Press.

Witte, John, Jr. 2002. *Law and Protestantism: The Legal Teachings of the Lutheran Reformation.* Cambridge: Cambridge University Press.

Wright, Benjamin F. 1931. *American Interpretations of Natural Law: A Study in the History of Political Thought*. Cambridge, Mass.: Harvard University Press.

Yarbrough, Tinsley E. 1988. *Mr. Justice Black and His Critics*. Durham, N.C.: Duke University Press.

Yudof, Mark G. 1979. "When Governments Speak: Toward a Theory of Government Expression and the First Amendment." *Texas Law Review* 57:863–918.

Zeisel, Hans. 1982. *The Limits of Law Enforcement*. Foreword by Edward H. Levi. Chicago: University of Chicago Press.

Indexes

Constitution

Creeds, Councils, and Confessions

Murdock v. *Pennsylvania* (1943), 64n
Murray's Lessee v. *Hoboken Land and Improvement Co.* (1856), 128n
Myers v. *United States* (1926), 31n

Near v. *Minnesota* (1931), 122n, 128n
New York Times Co. v. *Sullivan* (1964), 23n, 118–19, 132n
Nixon v. *Herndon* (1927), 65n

Palko v. *Connecticut* (1937), 132n
Pennsylvania Coal Co. v. *Mahon* (1922), 6n
Pierce v. *Society of Sisters* (1925), 110n
Plessy v. *Ferguson* (1896), 136–37, 142
Presser v. *Illinois* (1886), 107n
Public Utilities Commission v. *Pollak* (1952), 32

Rochin v. *California* (1952), 32n, 61n, 80n, 128n, 132n
Roth v. *United States* (1957), 67n, 69n

Scott v. *Sanford* [*Dred Scott*] (1857), 35, 119, 142
Slaughterhouse Cases (1873), 58
Smith v. *Allwright* (1944), 65n, 142n

The Thomas Jefferson (1825), 102n

United States v. *Booth* (1859), 10n, 23n, 54n, 88n, 89n, 110n, 119n, 142n
United States v. *Butler* (1936), 11n, 142
United States v. *Carolene Products Co.* (1938), 60n
United States v. *Cruikshank et al.* (1876), 20n, 107n

Weems v. *United States* (1910), 9n, 131n

Yick Wo v. *Hopkins* (1886), 131n

Zorach v. *Clauson* (1952), 7n, 20n

Proper Names

Ackerman, Bruce A., 24, 35
Aristotle, 29–30, 37, 53
Arius, 62
Arnold, Richard, 48
Arnold, Thurman, 135
Atatürk, Kemal, 18
Augustine, 62, 77, 147–48

Bach, Johann Sebastian, 96–97
Bengel, Johann Albrecht, 52–53
Berman, Harold J., 36
Black, Charles, 49
Black, Hugo Lafayette, 54–55, 81, 98, 132
Blackmun, Harry Andrew, 11n
Blackstone, William, 53–54, 124, 143
Blaustein, Albert P., 7

216 Indexes

Valla, Lorenzo, 100–101, 104

Waite, Morrison Remick, 20n, 106–7
Warren, Earl, 73, 74, 136–37
White, Byron Raymond, 49, 84, 100n, 102n
Whittaker, Charles Evans, 65

Williams, David C., 107
Wilson, James, 22–23
Wimsatt, William K., Jr., 93–94
Witte, John, Jr., 36
Woods, William Burnham, 107

Zwingli, Ulrich, 101–2